Fear of Persuasion

A New Perspective on
Advertising and Regulation

John E Calfee

A *Focus-on-Issues* book by AGORA in collaboration with The AEI Press

Published and distribute
Agora Association
PO Box 13, CH-1125 Monnaz, Switzerland
E-mail: books@agora-forum.org
Tel: +41-21-803-5014
Fax: +41-21-803-5008

Distributed in North America by
The AEI Press
c/o Publisher Resources Inc
1224 Heil Quaker Blvd
PO Box 7001, La Vergne, TN 37086-7001
Tel: 1-800-269-6267 / 1-800-937-6267
Fax: 1-800-774-6733

The views expressed in publications of AGORA are those of the authors and do not necessarily reflect the views of the members and officers of the AGORA Association.

Book design and production by Rupert Brown
Typesetting by Tom Carter Typography
Printed and bound in the UK

Swiss National Library, Bern, Switzerland
ISBN 2-940124-02-7
ISSN 1023-778 X

Library of Congress Cataloging-in-Publication Data
Calfee, John E., 1941 -
    Fear of persuasion : a new perspective on advertising and
regulation / John E. Calfee.
        p. cm.
    Includes bibliographical references.
    ISBN 2-940124-02-7 (alk. paper)
    1. Advertising. 2. Advertising – Psychological aspects.
    3. Persuasion (Psychology) 4. Advertising – Law and legislation
    – United States. I. Title.
    HF5821.C148 1997
    659. 1'01'9–dc21

                                                        97-37977
                                                            CIP

This book is dedicated to my mother,
Rhoda Baum Calfee
whose beneficial influence on all things of importance in my life,
most particularly including intellectual matters,
has been greater than she realizes.

Acknowledgements

My first debt is to my wife, Brenda, who patiently supplied her usual bounty of intellectual and emotional support throughout this project.

This book owes its existence to the efforts of Tana Wells and her over-achieving group, Agora. I could say that Tana harassed, cajoled, wheedled and threatened until the job was done, and then did the editing besides. All of that would be true, but beside the point.

Tana recognized that some important truths about advertising were too little noted by those who count, which is to say, consumers, advertisers and regulators. What was needed was an international perspective drawing on the latest research. She was certainly correct. The reader can decide whether this book meets that need.

Finally, my thanks to Randolp Stempski and Tericke Blanchard of the American Enterprise Institute for their tireless and intelligent research support.

Contents

Foreword

A few years ago, while researching a column, I ran across an article that had been published in 1986 in the journal *Regulation*. It was one of those rare pieces of writing that refute conventional wisdom utterly and let you see the world in an entirely different light.

In the article, 'The Ghost of Cigarette Advertising Past,' the author, John E Calfee, showed how heated advertising competition among cigarette makers actually drove tobacco sales *down* in the early 1950s. Sales perked up again in 1955 after the Federal Trade Commission stopped the ads because, it ruled, there was no proof to back up the claims made by the companies.

What were those claims? That smoking can kill you.

The main policy implication of the article was stunning: one good way to discourage smoking is to allow purveyors of cigarettes to talk about them freely to potential customers. Of course, the 1997 tobacco settlement does precisely the opposite, outlawing health claims and cartoon characters and requiring huge bureaucratic warnings on packs.

Tobacco is only one of many subjects treated in the book you hold in your hands. For example, Jack Calfee, who has become my colleague just down the hall at the American Enterprise Institute, also tackles children's toys – and he tells another story with a counter-intuitive lesson: television ads for toys actually lead to lower prices! Yes, children asked their parents to buy the toys they saw on TV, not caring about the cost, and the parents went to stores looking for the brands their kids wanted. 'A lot of people might assume that the parents encountered higher prices,' Calfee writes, 'because demand had been increased through advertising targeted at an ignorant audience [children].' But no. The ads boosted competition at the retail level, 'so much so that parents in search of heavily advertised toys actually found lower prices.' Driving down prices is one of the indirect benefits of advertising that Calfee describes in the book. Another is spreading information about health, which brings us back to the tobacco story…

Calfee writes that 'the first persuasive medical reports on smoking and lung cancer… created a phenomenal stir among smokers and the public generally. People who do not understand how advertising works would probably assume that cigarette manufacturers used advertising to divert attention away from the cancer reports. In fact, they did the opposite.'

Advertising to instill fear in the hearts of smokers blossomed, as manufacturers stuck filters on their cigarettes and cast aspersions on competitors that didn't. Kent, for example, claimed it 'takes out more nicotine and tars than any other leading cigarette – the difference in protection is priceless.' Unstated, of course, is that the priceless thing at stake here is your life. And, while the fear ads caused brand switching, they also frightened millions of Americans into stopping altogether. Sales fell by three percent in 1953 and by six percent in 1954.

'Never again,' writes Jack Calfee, 'not even in the face of the most impassioned anti-smoking publicity by the US Surgeon General or Food and Drug Administration, would cigarette consumption decline as rapidly as it did during these years of entirely market-driven anti-smoking advertising claims.'

Why? Simply because, presented with facts presented in a compelling fashion, consumers will tend to do the intelligent thing. Which is the theme of this book.

Of course, it's not so simple. At the heart of Jack Calfee's thesis is a delicious paradox: People don't believe what ads say, but they use ads all the time to get valuable information. In other words, people are properly skeptical; they take the self-interested claims they glean from ads and test them against the real world. Goods and services must measure up. If they don't, then, as the saying goes, 'nothing will kill a bad product quicker than good advertising' – a lesson I learned to my own chagrin when I served as a consultant for a new weekly newspaper in Washington. Great ads, mediocre (and soon, dead) product.

What the paradox shows is that advertising is part of a process – 'a self-enforcing mechanism, driven by competition and the profit motive in the face of enduring consumer skepticism.' In the end, advertisers can't persuade unless their products are credible, consistently meeting the demands of customers.

Even 10-year-old children fully understand the purpose of advertising and have 'an active suspicion of what advertisers say.' So why the fear of persuasion that comprises the title of this book? 'Advertising,' writes Jack Calfee, 'is always under attack' – by politicians, 'consumer advocates', and entrenched businesses that would prefer to live without the competition.

The attacks shouldn't come as a surprise. Each of these groups sees advertising as a threat to its own well being, or at the very least, an easy target to exploit. What Jack Calfee provides is a brilliant antidote to the fear-mongering and a compelling story, delivered with directness and wit.

As he will tell you shortly, the truth about advertising is that 'ads represent the seller's interest, consumers know this, and sellers know that consumers know it.' With such general enlightenment, why do we need busybodies to protect us?

James K Glassman
DeWitt-Wallace Reader's Digest Fellow in Communications
at the American Enterprise Institute and columnist for the *Washington Post*.

Introduction

'Advertising, it must be remembered, is a sort of fungus, a parasitic growth, adding no value to the goods consumed, and producing in general no direct return' [1]

'Advertising is under fire. Its adverse critics come from many camps and their complaints tend to become increasingly vehement ...' [2]

'The attack on advertising comes from all sectors' [3]

There are three great truths about advertising. First, advertising seeks to persuade and everyone knows it. The typical ad tries to induce a consumer to do one particular thing – usually, buy a product – instead of a thousand other things. There is nothing obscure about this purpose or what it means for buyers. Decades of data and centuries of intuition reveal that all consumers everywhere are deeply suspicious of what advertisers say and why they say it. This skepticism, far from representing an irrational fear or a barrier to creative advertising techniques, is in fact the driving force that makes advertising so effective. The persuasive purpose of advertising and the skepticism with which it is met are two sides of a single process. Like supply and demand (neither able to work alone, as in the famous analogy to two blades of a scissors), persuasion and skepticism work in tandem so advertising can do its job in competitive markets. Hence the first, multi-layered truth about advertising: ads represent the seller's self-interest, consumers know this, and sellers know that consumers know it.

The second great truth is that advertising is a tool for communicating information and shaping markets. It is one of the forces that compel sellers

---

[1] Frederick Dwight (1909) 'The Significance of Advertising', in the *Yale Review.*

[2] Neil Borden (1942) *The Economic Effects of Advertising*, Richard D Irwin, p 3.

[3] Theodore Levitt (1970) 'The Morality (?) of Advertising', *Harvard Business Review*, July–August.

to cater to the desires of consumers. Almost everyone knows this, too, because consumers use advertising every day, and they miss advertising when they cannot get it. This fact does not keep politicians and opinion leaders from routinely dismissing the value of advertising. But the truth is that people find advertising very useful indeed. The paradoxical fact that consumers obtain immense amounts of information from a process in which the providers of information are blatantly self-interested and the recipients are fundamentally skeptical, is one of the themes of this book.

This brings us to the third great truth. Advertising is always under attack – by politicians, by people who call themselves consumer advocates, by all sorts of scholarly groups (almost always people who study health or health advocacy, but not advertising or economics) and sometimes even by businesses who believe they would be better off in a world with less advertising. The words quoted at the start of this chapter were published in 1909, 1942 and 1970, but I could easily have found similar remarks from just about anytime in the past hundred years or more. In nearly all countries at nearly all times, I would venture to say, advertising is under popular and political attack.

These attacks on advertising are ironic in the extreme. The essence of persuasion is the absence of coercion. However dubious the concept of persuasion may be in other contexts (where the state controls the mass media, for example), anyone familiar with advertising as a business can affirm that consumers do not have to do what ads tell them to do, and that most ads are disputed, resented or ignored. The idea that society should collectively fear such blatant attempts at persuasion supplies the title of this book and could serve as a capsule summary of public policy debates over advertising.

This book is motivated by the third truth, the persistent attempt to blame advertising for much of what is wrong in society, and to fix these wrongs by regulating or prohibiting advertising. Part of the book is about regulation, as it must be in a world where regulation of advertising is pervasive, and where ad bans have been implemented or proposed for cigarettes, alcoholic beverages, prescription drugs, toys, all advertising directed at children, and numerous other products and categories.

The real subject of this book, however, is the constant, subtle dialogue between advertisers and consumers, and in parallel, the highly public battle between the freedom to communicate and the political urge to fix upon advertising as a scapegoat. To a substantial degree, the fate of advertising and its benefits rest upon the extent to which politicians, governments and the citizenry gain a better understanding of what advertising does, how it does it, and not least important, what advertising does not do. What follows is an attempt to advance that understanding.

1 Advertising and Competition

'[T]he [FTC advertising regulation] program over time has become firmly based on a set of longstanding principles that the Commission began developing in the 1970s. At the core is a recognition of the important role that advertising plays in the competitive process, and an understanding that unnecessary restraints on truthful advertising can be as harmful to consumers as deceptive or unfair advertising.' [4]

Much of this book is about getting the right answers to questions that are usually swamped with wrong answers. Let's begin with an easy one. Does advertising make competition work better? There is no doubt that advertising helps *competitors*. But the real question is whether advertising makes the competitive process work better for *consumers*. If advertising serves competition (and not just competitors), it expands the benefits of competition: better products, lower prices, and superior information.

So, does advertising serve competition? Of course it does. We know that today, on the basis of several decades of economic research. That research will be discussed shortly. But first, some historical perspective will be useful. It seems that advertising has not always been a favorite child of economists.

Old Thinking About Advertising and Competition

The giants of the 18th and 19th centuries, starting with Adam Smith and continuing through David Ricardo, Robert Malthus and John Stuart Mill, ignored advertising. By the beginning of the twentieth century, a more sympathetic view of advertising emerged from business economists, who taught in business schools and immersed themselves in the details

---

[4] Remarks of Robert Pitofsky, Chairman, Federal Trade Commission, before the American Advertising Federation Government Affairs Conference, 14 March, 1996, Washington, DC.

of business practice. Their work seems to have obtained relatively little notice among mainstream academicians, however.

A partial exception to this bleak outlook was the always sensible Cambridge economist Alfred Marshall (teacher of John Maynard Keynes, who sought to overturn much of what Marshall taught him). In his classic book, *Industry and Trade*, Marshall briefly analyzed the role of advertising. To be sure, he endorsed the then common view that much, if not most, advertising was wasteful. But he also recognized that advertising was essential for new products. His example was the typewriter: 'When the idea of a typewriter was first conceived, very few people were inclined to take seriously the suggestion that it could rival the pen in efficiency.' Advertising helped to overcome this information deficit. Marshall concluded that advertising could enable consumers to 'satisfy their wants without inordinate fatigue or loss of time.'[5]

Marshall also provided a short but remarkably insightful summary of the new discipline of market research, which even in those days borrowed heavily from the young science of psychology. He observed that 'the task [of measuring the effects of advertising] is more difficult than appears at first sight [and]... the attainment of trustworthy general results seems yet far off.'[6] That prediction has held up rather well. Even today, we should view with suspicion any claim that advertisers can use psychology to create advertising that is certain to sell products.

Alfred Marshall notwithstanding, many of the most famous economists of the first half of the twentieth century were strongly critical of advertising. The list includes the notable British scholars A C Pigou, E H Chamberlain, and Joan Robinson. All argued that advertising was inherently wasteful, or worse. They thought advertising distorted consumer information and preferences, and was a tool for creating or buttressing monopoly power. These economists were deeply suspicious of competitive markets generally. It is entirely characteristic of their views that they saw advertising as a means for subverting competition. They devised elaborate

---

[5] See Alfred Marshall (1920) *Industry and Trade*, London: MacMillan, p 304. The quote on satisfying wants is from Robert B Ekelund, Jr, and David S Saurman (1988) *Advertising and the Market Process*, Pacific Research Institute for Public Policy, p 19.

[6] See Marshall (1920), *ibid*, p 307, on market research.

theoretical reasoning to support the idea that if governments did not intervene, manufacturers would create meaningless distinctions among brands and would then use advertising to create artificial demand for these 'differentiated' products. In their eyes, every large advertiser was a monopolist of some sort, and clever advertisers would figure out ways to deprive consumers of the benefits that should arise from competitive markets.[7]

This reasoning was new in its details, but old in spirit. It reflected a centuries-old view of advertising as a dark force that overwhelms consumers through sheer persuasion. As long ago as 1759, the famous writer, lexicographer and conversationalist Samuel Johnson declared that 'The trade of advertising is now so near to perfection, it is not easy to propose any improvement. But as every art ought to be exercised in due subordination to the publick good, I cannot but propose it as a mere question to these matters of the publick ear. Whether they do not sometimes play too wantonly with our passions. [sic]'[8] The assumption that progress in advertising science was a bad thing for consumers took more or less permanent possession of the minds of a goodly portion of the educated public. One consequence is that best-seller lists frequently contain books with titles like *Hidden Persuaders*, amounting to little more than unrestrained attacks on advertising as having nearly unlimited power over consumers.[9]

This deeply mistaken view of advertising has been a frequent source of mischief. For one thing, it led governments to place an astonishing faith in the power of propaganda. After all, as the scholar Raymond Bauer noted forty years ago, the 'specter of "manipulation" and "hidden persuasion" has stalked all the lands that man has ever inhabited.' Governments beset by crises were tempted to harness the supposed power of mass persuasion to boost morale and divert the citizenry. During World War I, governments on both sides employed crude forms of propaganda, which of course is just

---

7 *Cf* Ekelund and Saurman (1988), *op cit*, pp 20ff.

8 Quote taken from George Burton Hotchkiss (1940) *Outline of Advertising: Its Philosophy, Science, Art and Strategy*, New York: MacMillan, p 40.

9 Packard, Vance (1957) *Hidden Persuaders*, D McKay Co.

government advertising on a massive scale. These propaganda campaigns largely failed, however, a fact that was apparent to scholars and others when they examined the results after the war was over.[10]

Looking back on the failure of propaganda, the democracies learned their lessons fairly well. When another world crisis arrived in the form of World War II, the so-called propaganda by the Western Allies was far more restrained and realistic in its expectations about what could be achieved by unalloyed persuasion.

The socialist nations, however, completely missed the point. For decades after 1917, the Russian Soviet Union and other communist nations employed propaganda on an unprecedented scale. They operated under the illusion that the most obvious capitalist tool of all – advertising – had a power it never had. One can only imagine the astonishment of these authorities when their systems collapsed and they discovered that after decades of massive anti-capitalist 'education,' Russian consumers thought about markets much as consumers in other nations did. They had (and continue to have) the same deep suspicion of advertising (especially in the late 1980s before Russians had gained much firsthand experience with Western advertising), but they also had the same almost instinctive ability to turn advertising to their own purposes. And of course, the propaganda left little if any faith in the centrally planned economic systems whose virtues were incessantly pressed upon the populace.[11]

The idea that advertising is the consumer's natural enemy persisted through most of the twentieth century. In the 1930s, when capitalism was in crisis throughout the West and the 'consumer movement' was born, advertising was a convenient scapegoat. When capitalism triumphed in the West in the 1950s, advertising was depicted as capitalism's weak link,

---

[10] The quote and much of the discussion here is taken from the penetrating analysis in Raymond A Bauer (1958) 'Limits of Persuasion: The Hidden Persuaders Are Made of Straw', 36/5 *Harvard Business Review* (September).

[11] See Robert Shiller, Maxim Boycko, and Vladimir Korobov (1991) 81/3 *American Economic Review*, pp 385–400. Analyzing the results from identical telephone interviews in May 1990, they concluded that American and Soviet respondents were 'basically similar in some very important dimensions: in their attitudes toward fairness, income inequality, and incentives and in their understanding of the working of markets.' On international attitudes toward advertising, see the discussion in the section on consumer skepticism in chapter 2.

an unwelcome force standing in the way of economic progress. An intense intellectual debate raged over whether advertising was a good thing at all. Anti-advertising rhetoric seems to have reached a peak in best-selling books such as Vance Packard's *Hidden Persuaders* and John Kenneth Galbraith's *The Affluent Society*. Both propounded the idea that advertising was largely a subversive force that leaves consumers worse off than they would have been with no advertising at all.

New Evidence and New Thinking About Advertising and Consumers

In the 1950s and 1960s, economists launched a wave of detailed empirical research on advertising. This research did not examine how the information in advertising actually affects markets. Rather, it focused on one specific question: is advertising a 'barrier to entry,' that is to say, an anticompetitive force that buttresses inferior products and inhibits entry by superior ones. This research enterprise would finally put to the test the most basic of the intellectual attacks on advertising in the 1930s.

Scholars approached the issue of monopoly power from several angles, looking at the connections between advertising and, say, profits, or the number of sellers in a particular industry, or the rate at which new sellers entered the market. Much was learned about how to measure such things as profits, market shares, and even technological innovation. But learning how advertising could actually bolster monopoly proved unexpectedly difficult. As academic scrutiny intensified, the apparent connections between advertising and monopoly power largely disappeared. In fact, the evidence tended toward the view that advertising actually facilitated entry by new products and firms. In short, a decade or two of research failed to uncover a tendency for advertising to impede competition. Advertising's supposed power to maintain monopolies turned out to be something of an academic will-of-the-wisp.[12]

Then a relatively new school of economic analysis arrived on the scene, marshalling theoretical and empirical evidence on the benefits

---

[12] An excellent overview of older and modern economic views of advertising can be found in Ekelund and Saurman (1988), *op cit*. Less theoretical, with more emphasis on history and institutions, is Michael Schudson (1986 paperback edition) *Advertising: The Uneasy Persuasion*, Basic Books.

of advertising. Attention focused on the information in advertising, on consumers' instinctive dismissal of unsubstantiated claims, and on the amazing resourcefulness of advertisers in using brands to establish credibility with consumers. The 'advertising as information' school of thought joined together with the new economics of competition and regulation.

Much of this new thinking came under the rubric of the 'Chicago school' of economics, famous for its emphasis on the virtues of competitive markets and the flaws of government regulation. Future Nobel laureate George Stigler provided an early start in his pioneering 1961 article, 'the Economics of Information,' which argued that 'advertising is an immensely powerful instrument for the elimination of ignorance.' [13] In the 1960s and 1970s, the Chicago school (by no means located exclusively within the University of Chicago itself) began producing compelling explanations of how advertising improves markets.[14]

They explained why competing sellers have incentives to provide price and other information for consumers to use for their own purposes, even if those purposes included the extraction of better bargains from sellers. It was shown that competitive advertising can yield potent benefits to virtually all consumers even when only a relatively small proportion of buyers actually go to the trouble to educate themselves about the prices and quality of competing brands.

Similar reasoning explained how sellers can use advertising to signal that they have a stake in maintaining product quality and consumer satisfaction (because otherwise the advertising would be largely wasted). Even such apparently uninformative techniques as massive 'image' advertising for soft drinks could in fact provide powerful quality signals to consumers. The logic was simple but compelling: most products are

---

[13] George Stigler (1961) 'The Economics of Information', 69 *Journal of Political Economy*, pp 213–225.

[14] Basic sources on the 'new economics' of antitrust and regulation (including advertising regulation) during the 1970s include Harvey, Goldschmid, ed. (1974) *Industrial Concentration: The New Learning*, Boston: Little, Brown; David G Tuerck, ed. *Issues in Advertising: the Economics of Persuasion*, Washington: American Enterprise Institute; and Kenneth Clarkson and Timothy J Muris, eds (1981) *The Federal Trade Commission since 1970: Economic Regulation and Bureaucratic Behavior*, New York: Cambridge University Press.

profitable only through repeat sales. If an ad induces people to try a brand, it pays off for the seller only if new buyers are sufficiently satisfied to keep on buying. This means that profits from advertising for brands that satisfy consumers are greater than for brands that disappoint buyers. This induces advertising to gravitate toward better brands. Consumers, being on the whole a smart bunch on the alert for new bargains, soon catch on.[15]

The implication is that even the types of advertising most criticized as wasteful are far more useful than analysts had realized. The old saying among advertising professionals – 'nothing kills a bad product faster than good advertising' – was finally demonstrated in a rigorous fashion. Of course, the essential role of brand names as a guarantee of quality had been clear to businessmen for centuries; now economic thinking was catching up and was providing a solid theoretical foundation for the role of brand advertising. Parallel work by consumer researchers helped to establish these principles in the academic literature and in teaching.[16]

Empirical research on advertising, information, prices and product quality fit well with the emerging theories. Almost all of this examined American markets. A pioneering study compared the prices of eyeglasses in states that either permitted or restricted advertising for eyeglass services. Prices were about 25% higher where advertising was restricted or banned (and prices were highest for the least educated consumers). A later study by the Federal Trade Commission (FTC) staff showed that product quality in the states without advertising was *not* higher despite

---

[15] On the latter point, see Amna Kirmani and Peter Wright (1989) 'Money Talks: Perceived Advertising Expense and Expected Product Quality', 16/3 *Journal of Consumer Research*, pp 344–353; and the very interesting article in *The Economist*, 29 February 1992, p 75, 'The Medium Is the Message'. Two useful sources on the 'new economics' of advertising are Yale Brozen, ed, (1974), *Advertising and Society*, New York: New York University Press; and Philip Nelson (1974) 'Advertising as Information', 82 *Journal of Political Economy*, p 729. Much of the new theoretical reasoning was reviewed by three scholars who were then members of the FTC staff: Howard Beales, Richard Craswell, and Stephen Salop (1981) 'The Efficient Regulation of Consumer Information', *Journal of Law and Economics*, Vol.24, pp 491–539 (December). A more recent development of additional theory on market information and signals is by the FTC staff economist Pauline Ippolito (1990) 'Bonding and Non-Bonding Signal of Product Quality', 63/1, pt.1 *Journal of Business*, pp 41–60.

[16] An excellent textbook that blends economic thinking with the more psychological approaches to consumer behavior is William L Wilkie (1989) *Consumer Behavior*, New York: J Wiley and Sons.

the higher prices.[17] Studies also found higher prices in the absence of advertising for such diverse products as gasoline, prescription drugs and legal services.[18] The extensive research on health claims for foods (reviewed in chapter 2) documented broad improvements in consumer information in connection with advertising, as well as changes in news coverage, consumer diets and even foods.

New Regulatory Principles at the FTC

The 1970s started out on a wave of anti-advertising sentiment. The idea that advertising needed new restraints dominated government circles and popular opinion. The FTC, which regulates most advertising, came under vigorous attack. Sources as diverse as the American Bar Association and consumer advocate Ralph Nader described the FTC as a sleepy agency that had failed to keep deceptive and unfair advertising from harming consumers. Stung by this criticism, the Nixon administration and Congress virtually recreated the FTC with new personnel and new legislation. The new laws (primarily the Magnuson-Moss amendments to the FTC Act) provided the FTC with explicit power to establish detailed rules on advertising, along with new powers to impose fines for violations of FTC orders and rules.[19]

[17] Lee Benham (1972) 'The Effect of Advertising on the Price of Eyeglasses', 15 *Journal of Law and Economics*, pp 337–352; and Lee Benham and A Benham (1975) 'Regulating through the Professions: A Perspective on Information Control', 18 *Journal of Law and Economics,* pp 421–447 (October). The FTC studies were Ronald Bond, John Kwoka, Jr, John Phelan and Ira Taylor Whitten (1980) *Staff Report on Effects of Restrictions on Advertising and Commercial Practice in the Professions: The Case of Optometry,* Bureau of Economics, Federal Trade Commission; and John Kwoka (1984) 'Advertising and Price and Quality of Optometric Services', 74 *American Economic Review,* pp 211–216.

[18] On gasoline, see A Maurizi and T Kelly (1978) *Prices and Consumer Information: The Benefits from Posting Retail Gasoline Prices,* Washington, DC: American Enterprise Institute. On prescription drugs, see J F Cady (1972) 'An Estimation of the Price Effects of Restrictions on Drug Price Advertising', 14 *Economic Inquiry,* pp 493–511; and J Howard Beales (1996) 'New Uses for Old Drugs', in Robert Helms, ed, *Competitive Strategies in the Pharmaceutical Industry,* Washington, DC: American Enterprise Institute, pp 281–305. On legal services, see John Schroeter, Scott Smith and Steven Cox (1987) 'Advertising and Competition in Routine Legal Service Markets: An Empirical Investigation', 35 *Journal of Industrial Economics,* p 49; and Federal Trade Commission (1984) *Improving Consumer Access to Legal Services: The Case for Removing Restrictions on Truthful Advertising,* Staff Report by William W Jacobs, *et al.*

[19] See American Bar Association (1969) *Report of the American Bar Association Commission to Study the Federal Trade Commission,* Washington, DC: American Bar Association; and Edward F Cox, Robert C Fellmeth, and John E Schulz (1969) *Nader's Raiders: Report on the Federal Trade Commission,* New York: Grove Press. Clarkson and Muris, eds (1981), *op cit.,* provides a convenient set of articles on the FTC in the 1970s.

In this manner, an extravagantly praised 'new' FTC was born. It quickly constructed detailed rules for mail order sales and for sales of many individual products including electronic amplifiers, home insulation, funerals, and used cars. The FTC also dramatically escalated its regulation of advertising. It conducted a series of 'rounds' in which every seller in various markets was required to turn over voluminous materials. The FTC staff reviewed these materials in order to determine whether advertising claims relied upon sufficient evidence. The agency also required firms to make supporting materials available for public scrutiny. The idea was that outside individuals and groups (such as consumer activists) would quickly sift through the evidence and reveal to the public which ad claims had been made without adequate support. These files just gathered dust.

The FTC soon adopted a different policy toward advertising claims by establishing its 'advertising substantiation' doctrine. This required firms to possess what the FTC regarded as a 'reasonable basis' for all claims, but it did not require firms to submit any materials unless the FTC asked for them (which the agency has often done). This represented a substantial tightening of FTC regulation. Previously, the FTC had to demonstrate that claims were false; now it could require firms to demonstrate that their claims were true.[20]

A related development was also important. During these same years, the advertising community devised a self-regulation system run by the Better Business Bureau. This system fielded complaints from consumers (and more often, from competitors), resolved disputes and when necessary (which was not often) sent unresolved cases to the FTC. The television broadcasters also put together a comprehensive self-regulation scheme. Similar developments occurred in the United Kingdom and some European nations, and the advertising self-regulation movement in its diverse forms now spans most of the world. It merits a chapter of its own (see chapter 6).

---

[20] The events in this and the preceding paragraph are described in a useful but neglected FTC staff memo, 'Evolution and Evaluation of the Ad Substantiation Program since 1971', 1 December 1978, by Collot Guerard and Julie Niemasik. A more widely available account by the present chairman of the FTC is Robert Pitofsky (1977) 'Beyond Nader: Consumer Protection and the Regulation of Advertising', 90 *Harvard Law Review,* pp 661–701.

All this amounted to a new regulatory regime far more powerful than anything seen since the advent of mass media advertising in the nineteenth century. One might think that this was simply another advance in the harnessing of intellectual and legal forces to the task of exerting control over advertising. No doubt, many critics of advertising saw it very much in those terms. But this time the tables were turned.

It turned out that the FTC and the US courts were paying remarkably close attention to the new economic thinking on advertising. Economists and economically minded lawyers on the FTC staff were working directly with independent scholars, many of them consumer researchers on loan to the FTC from university appointments. They provided an effective combination of expertise and practical policy recommendations.[21]

The result was a new era of government activism on advertising in the United States – but with an amazing new twist. In an odd congruence of political and intellectual forces, the new consumer protection joined with the new economic analysis of advertising to produce a surprising mix of policies toward advertising. The FTC began to adopt policies fundamentally sympathetic to advertising and to the freedom to advertise.

The new regulatory posture had three basic components. First, the FTC revised its notions of what kinds of advertising are deceptive. To start things off, the agency simply abandoned some common kinds of advertising deception litigation that had proved to be anti-consumer. The most striking examples were the so-called 'fictitious pricing' cases. These involved ads that referred to 'list prices,' 'regular prices,' '20% off regular price,' and the like. For decades, the FTC had argued that such ads were practically always deceptive because it was impossible to fully monitor competitors' prices, and the advertiser itself often made relatively few sales

---

21 An example is the fascinating 1979 FTC staff report, *Consumer Information Remedies*, which emanated from one of a series of 'Policy Review Sessions' that brought together academics and FTC personnel at the very peak of regulatory activism under Chairman Michael Pertschuk. Insightful examples of the application of consumer research and economics to practical regulatory issues are William L Wilkie (1986) 'Affirmative Disclosure at the FTC: Objectives for the Remedy and Outcomes of Past Orders' 4 *Journal of Public Policy and Marketing*, pp 91–111; and Richard Craswell (1985) 'Interpreting Deceptive Advertising', 65 *Boston University Law Review*, pp 657–732. A valuable collection of memoirs and historical pieces is Patrick Murphy and William L Wilkie, eds (1990) *Marketing and Advertising Regulation: The Federal Trade Commission in the 1990s*, University of Notre Dame Press.

at its own 'regular' price. This kind of advertising is the subject of a short case study in chapter 7, but it is useful to review here the evolution of FTC policy.

Cheered on by high-priced shops and department stores, the FTC made fictitious price cases the single most common form of advertising litigation during the 1950s and 1960s. In theory, the FTC was protecting consumers from deception. In practice, it was keeping prices high by repeatedly suing the price-cutters. Those were mainly newer and more efficient retailers who charged lower prices and wanted to use advertising to tell consumers about their own prices and their competitors' higher prices.

Eventually, the FTC realized that it was working against the consumer's interest. When it overhauled its consumer protection policies in the early 1970s, the FTC openly and permanently ceased bringing fictitious pricing cases.[22] These cases are now rare in the US, although they are occasionally pursued by individual states (fortunately with little practical effect). Unfortunately, the story is very different in other nations. Germany, for example, is notorious for its hostility to anything resembling a comparative price claim.

The FTC also modified its policies on deceptive advertising in general. This change, too, strongly reflected the new thinking about the benefits of advertising and the ways in which consumers actually use advertising. The policy shift occupied perhaps a decade and a half. During the 1970s, the FTC staff gradually dismantled its traditional policy of attacking ads that would deceive only the most gullible consumers. In particular, the FTC abandoned the assumption that a claim is deceptive if it possesses the 'tendency' or even the 'capacity' to deceive a small segment of consumers.

The new policy was crystallized in two formal statements. The 'Policy Statement on Deception,' issued in 1983, described general principles, with emphasis on the 'reasonable consumer' and the importance of actual

---

[22] An excellent more or less contemporary source on FTC policies is a much-cited article by Robert Pitofsky, who implemented this policy switch as Director of the Bureau of Consumer Protection, helped enforce it in the late 1970s and early 1980s as a member of the FTC, and is now Chairman of the FTC. See Robert Pitofsky (1977), *op cit.* A more recent update in this area by two FTC staff economists is Ronald S Bond and R Dennis Murphy (1992) 'An Analysis of Department Store Reference Pricing in Metropolitan Washington', Bureau of Economics, Federal Trade Commission, September 1992.

or likely consumer injury (rather than the theoretical possibility of harm).
The policies set forth in the 1983 statement aroused controversy, but they
have proved remarkably resilient under three Presidents from both political
parties.[23] The far less controversial 'Advertising Substantiation Policy
Statement' of 1984 explained the Commission's 'reasonable basis' standard
for advertising claims. That standard takes into account a variety of factors
including the potential harm from claims that turn out to be false, potential
benefits from true claims, and the costs of providing more definitive
substantiation for claims.[24]

The two FTC statements of the early 1980s ruled out the possibility
of imposing blanket prohibitions on such beneficial techniques as
comparative advertising, and they permitted useful claims to go forward
even if it was impossible to demonstrate that the claims were absolutely
certain to be true. The statements also recognized the self-correcting role
of competitive forces (in connection with inexpensive frequently purchased
products, for example). The result was to permit a large body of useful
advertising (such as health claims for foods and those 'fictitious price'
claims) that in the decades before 1970 would have been suppressed
on the grounds that someone, somewhere might have gotten the wrong
impression.

The second component of the FTC's new advertising policy was
to seek to dismantle barriers against advertising. The agency began to take
action against government agencies and private groups that restricted
advertising. A special section of the legal staff (the 'Competition Advocacy
Program') was devoted to submitting 'intervention' statements to other
federal and state government agencies with the goal of persuading those

[23] Federal Trade Commission (1983) 'Deception Statement' ('Policy Statement on Deception'),
45 *Antitrust and Trade Regulation Report* 689, 27 October 1983; reprinted as an appendix to
FTC v Cliffdale Associates, Inc, et al, 103 FTC 110, pp 174–184 (1984). The genesis and contents of the
deception statement are analyzed in Gary T Ford and John E Calfee (1986) 'Recent Developments in
FTC Policy on Deception', 50 *Journal of Marketing,* (July) pp 82–103. Another useful summary of
developments, with special attention to the harm that has arisen when the individual states have stuck
with older policies, can be found in J Howard Beales and Timothy J Muris (1993) *State and Federal
Regulation of National Advertising,* Washington, DC: The AEI Press.

[24] Federal Trade Commission (1984) 'Advertising Substantiation Policy Statement', 47 *Antitrust and
Trade Regulation Report,* pp 234–235, 2 August 1984, and appended to *Thompson Medical Company,*
104 *FTC* 648, pp 839–942 (1984).

agencies to reduce restrictions on advertising. This thankless attempt at a particularly challenging line of persuasion continues to this day as FTC economists and lawyers offer their intuition and expertise to other agencies with less confidence in the benefits of advertising.[25]

The FTC lawyers also attacked advertising restrictions by private groups. One by one, professional organizations of physicians, psychologists, and even lawyers buckled under FTC pressure to end so-called 'ethical' prohibitions on advertising. As the FTC staff pointed out, these prohibitions were motivated almost entirely by a desire to reduce competition, especially price competition. The FTC also used its influence to end prohibitions on comparative advertising on television, and to curtail anti-competitive aspects of the broadcast networks' codes on toy advertising.[26]

This new view of advertising regulation recently combined with antitrust regulation to obtain striking results. In 1994, the FTC obtained an order prohibiting manufacturers of baby formula from agreeing *not* to advertise. A number of states and groups of formula purchasers had also sued these firms. The main charge was that these firms, supported by the leading pediatricians' organization, established an industry self-regulation code that prohibited advertising to consumers. The effect was to discourage entry by Nestlé, which unlike other firms relied primarily upon consumer advertising. With Nestlé out of the picture, the industry was apparently able to engineer price increases. One of the offenders, Abbott Laboratories, agreed to pay $32.5 million to settle a number of cases.[27]

This was a remarkable development. While so-called consumer activists continually attacked advertising and promotion of infant formula

---

[25] See, for example, Federal Trade Commission, Bureau of Consumer Protection and Bureau of Economics, (1996) 'Comments to the Food and Drug Administration on Direct-to-Consumer Promotion of Prescription Drugs', 11 January 1996.

[26] The 1984 FTC staff report on lawyer advertising, by Jacobs, *et al, op cit,* contains some useful historical background. On the FTC's support for comparative advertising claims, see Ross Petty (1997) 'Advertising Law in the United States and European Union', 16/1 *Journal of Public Policy and Marketing,* pp 2–13, at p 7.

[27] The FTC case is *Abbott Laboratories,* Docket No 9253, (1994), FTC Lexis 42. Other lawsuits are described in *Wall Street Journal,* 28 May 1996, p A25, 'Abbot Agrees to Pay $32.5 Million to Settle Infant-Formula Case', by Thomas Burton.

as being unfair to consumers in many nations, consumer protection regulators in the US attacked manufacturers for seeking to *stop* infant formula advertising.

There is a third and less well-known component to the revolution in FTC advertising regulation that began in the 1970s. FTC economists and attorneys launched a series of empirical studies of advertising. This research has enriched the academic literature and supported new departures in FTC policy. For example, I have already noted that FTC economists performed some of the most careful research on advertising for eyeglass services. That led directly to an FTC rule that prohibited a variety of state-level restrictions on advertising and competition. Other FTC research has addressed price advertising, attorney advertising, and health claims for foods. The results have buttressed litigation and rulemaking, as well as the FTC's efforts to reduce unnecessary advertising restrictions by other agencies.[28]

The Merging of Research and Policy

These events did much to establish the modern view of advertising and advertising regulation. Two contrasting trends emerged more or less simultaneously. One was a series of political triumphs for the consumer protection movement. That usually means more regulation. But the other development was the emerging recognition that advertising is so valuable that restrictions on advertising can actually harm consumers. Modern consumer protection has therefore come to include a substantial measure of freedom to advertise.

The unexpected march away from stringent regulation of advertising culminated in a new era in 'First Amendment' law applying the US Constitution's 'freedom of speech' clause. Beginning in the mid-1970s, the US Supreme Court has provided substantial constitutional protection against legislated restraints on truthful advertising. Pro-advertising trends in constitutional law now extend far beyond the United States to include Canada and the European Union (EU). These extremely important developments are described in chapter 8 on advertising and freedom.

---

28 This research has been cited above or is cited in the discussion of health claims for foods in chapter 2.

Looking back on these two and half decades, the chairman of the FTC summed it up in the words quoted at the beginning of this chapter and repeated here: '[T]he [FTC advertising regulation] program over time has become firmly based on a set of longstanding principles that the Commission began developing in the 1970s. At the core is a recognition of the important role that advertising plays in the competitive process, and an understanding that unnecessary restraints on truthful advertising can be as harmful to consumers as deceptive or unfair advertising.' [29]

A similar view has taken hold in other nations and particularly in the EU, where Directorate General XV of the European Commission has taken up the task of preserving and expanding the freedom to advertise in order to promote the economic well-being of European consumers. The recent 'Green Paper' on commercial communication from the staff of DG XV stated, 'Commercial communications could benefit from the principle of freedom of expression as enshrined in Article 10(1) of the European Convention of Human Rights and in Article 19 of the International Covenant on Civil and Political Rights.'[30]

Scholarly thinking about advertising and regulation has come full circle. Advertising was once thought to be a source of monopoly power. Now even many government regulators recognize that it is ad *bans* that are the source of monopoly power.[31] Advertising was once seen as a fountain of misinformation and a tool for shaping the desires of compliant consumers. Now it is understood to be a tool for consumers to use for their own purposes, something to be welcomed rather than feared.

Underlying these shifts in intellectual perspective and regulatory law has been an emerging understanding of the subtle, complex and powerful relationships between advertising and consumer information. We have only touched upon that topic, which is next.

---

29 Pitofsky, 1996, *op cit.*

30 European Commission, *Commercial Communications in the Internal Market*, Brussels, 5 August 1996.

31 Again, FTC Chairman Robert Pitofsky, as quoted in an FTC Press Release, 1 August 1995: 'Advertising is a key source of price and other information and when competitors band together to restrict it, consumers lose.'

2 Advertising and Information: The Obvious and the Nonobvious

'No More Diphtheria' [32]

'425,000 Strokes Are Uncalled For' [33]

'... it's clear that despite all the billions advertisers spend to sway viewers and readers to buy their products, consumers are, at the very least, skeptical' [34]

Why does advertising provide information to consumers, and how does it do it? The answers provide the basis for understanding how advertising works and how regulation can and should work.

Why Advertising is Necessary for the Public Good – In Theory

Is advertising necessary? With so many other information sources available, is there any reason to use a medium that is expensive and whose claims are usually not taken at face value? One could imagine a world in which almost no information comes from advertising. Newspapers, magazines, handouts, and radio and television broadcasting could provide information about prices, sales, products, features, the importance of product characteristics (energy consumption, cholesterol content), new purchasing conditions (higher fuel prices), research findings (safety devices, nutrition), and so on – and they could do all this in ways that catch the eye and impress the minds of the relevant consumers.

---

32 Headline from a full-page ad run by Metropolitan Life Insurance, reproduced in Frank Presbrey (1929) *The History and Development of Advertising*, p 615. With subheadlines of 'Diphtheria can be stamped out!' and 'If you love them – Make them safe', the ad described the Schick test, which could test whether a child is immune to diphtheria or needs a vaccination.

33 Ad for Genentech, a pharmaceutical firm, in *New York Times*, 2 May 1997, and other newspapers. Genentech is the manufacturer of the first proven treatment for strokes.

34 *Wall Street Journal*, 'Consumers Say They Aren't Buying Advertisers' Hard Sell, Survey Finds', 14 July 1995.

But someone would have to pay for all this, not just for print space and broadcast air time, but also for collecting and packaging information, gauging consumer tastes and needs, and all the other necessities of effective information creation and dissemination. In theory, this is no problem. A lot of this information is worth more than it costs. So – again in theory – consumers would be willing to cover the costs, with the implication that this information could be collected, packaged and sold to consumers at a profit.

This assumes the existence of a system of property rights. For most products, this is provided by patents and copyrights. Everyone knows that if computer programs could be copied and distributed for free, they could not be sold at a price sufficient to pay for years of work by hundreds of programmers. That is why there is copyright protection for computer programs and other concrete forms of expression such as books, articles, pictures and diagrams.

But information itself can be neither patented nor copyrighted. Once the most important facts are put before the public – things like prices and comparisons between products – they can be copied and used and even disseminated to others, without compensating the original source of the information. Nor does the problem end there. What cannot be sold at a profit tends not to be created. With no property rights to pure information, anyone who arduously accumulates useful facts about product prices and features must be prepared to see his work appropriated without compensation as soon as it appears. Why expect people to pay for what they can get practically for free?

The fact that it is difficult or impossible to sell pure information for what it is worth is one of the most fundamental principles in modern economics. The implication is that much valuable information will not be created, and even if it is created, no one will pay the costs of disseminating the information through the mass media.

There is a solution, although not a perfect one. The solution is to arrange for the information to be so closely tied to the product that buyers will pay for the information as part of the price of the product.

Sometimes legal arrangements can make this work. Pharmaceuticals are an example (within limits). Hundreds of millions of dollars are required to develop and demonstrate to a government's satisfaction that a particular chemical entity can be used to treat a medical condition (the tally is roughly a quarter of a billion dollars on average in the United States in recent years). As a general rule, this high-priced bundle of information applies only to that one chemical. A patent keeps competitors from marketing the same chemical, so the price can be kept high enough to cover the costs of the information (including the costs of disseminating the information, which can be even higher than the development costs). Because the information applies only to this precise product, it is easy to cover the costs of information through sales of the product. The manufacturer has little reason to worry about others disseminating the information without compensation, because doing so will actually help the company (which after all has a monopoly).

Pharmaceuticals are a very special case, however. The carefully constructed web of patents and regulations that generate mountains of information about new drugs cannot be used for foods, automobiles, electronics and thousands of other staples of modern life. After all, new drugs are rare, whereas a well functioning market creates thousands of new products and product variations every year. For most products, the market itself must supply the necessary connections between products and information about products, without the help of the virtual monopolies generated by detailed regulation. What is needed is a way for the market to provide a payoff for disseminating valuable information even when it is impossible to get people to pay for the information directly.

This is where advertising comes in to help solve the information problem, a fact that is on display wherever advertising is permitted. Sellers use advertising to provide useful information that favors their own brands, and they cover the costs through higher prices or larger volumes. In effect, information and products are bound together into single bundle for a single price. This permits advertising to be a powerful vehicle for distributing information.

There is nothing new about this idea. For example, an article published in 1925 declared that 'I believe the time will come when people will ... recognize that the giving of information about goods and services is a service that somehow must be performed and must be paid for. If there is a better way of performing it than advertising, it has yet to be found.' [35]

Just how useful is this connection between advertising and information? At first blush, the process sounds rather limited. Volvo ads tell consumers that Volvos have side-impact air bags, people learn a little about the importance of air bags, and Volvo sells a few more cars. This seems to help hardly anyone except Volvo and its customers.

If advertising always provided such a narrow range of information, there would be little reason to celebrate it as a solution to the economic problems of information. But advertising does much more. It routinely provides immense amounts of information that benefits primarily parties *other* than the advertiser. This may sound odd, but it is a logical result of market forces and the nature of information itself.

The mere ability to use information to sell products is an incentive to create new information through research. Whether the topic is nutrition, safety or more mundane matters like how to measure amplifier power, the necessity of achieving credibility with consumers and critics requires much of this research to be placed in the public domain, and that it rest upon some academic credentials. That kind of research typically produces results that apply to more than just the brands sold by the firm sponsoring the research. The lack of property rights to pure information ensures that this extra information is available at no charge. Both consumers and competitors may borrow the new information for their own purposes.

Advertising also elicits additional information from other sources. Claims that are striking, original, forceful or even merely obnoxious will generate news stories about the claims, the controversies they cause, the reactions of competitors (a price war?, a splurge of comparison ads?), the reactions of consumers and the remarks of governments and independent authorities.

Here is how the process works in practice.

---

[35] George Burton Hotchkiss writing in the *American Economic Review*, (1925), as quoted by Presbrey, (1929), *op cit*, p 602.

Why Advertising is Necessary for the Public Good – In Practice

Probably the most concrete, pervasive and persistent example of competitive advertising that works for the public good is price advertising. Its effect is invariably to heighten competition and reduce prices, even the prices of firms that assiduously avoid mentioning prices in their own advertising. Unfortunately, this is also an area where government restrictions are common – so common, in fact, and so varied in their details, that price advertising forms a case study in chapter 7, which describes the most important regulatory implications of what we have learned about how advertising works.

There is another area where the public benefits of advertising are less obvious but equally important. The unremitting nature of consumer interest in health, and the eagerness of sellers to cater to consumer desires, guarantees that advertising related to health will provide a storehouse of telling observations on the ways in which the benefits of advertising extend beyond the interests of advertisers to include the interests of the public at large.

Case Study: Health Claims for Foods [36]

Here is what seems to be the best documented example of why advertising is necessary for consumer welfare. In the 1970s, public health experts described compelling evidence that people who eat more fiber are less likely to get cancer, especially cancer of the colon, which happens to be the second leading cause of deaths from cancer in the United States. By 1979, the US Surgeon General was recommending that people eat more fiber in order to prevent cancer.

Consumers appeared to take little notice of these recommendations, however. The National Cancer Institute, a branch of the US government's National Institutes of Health, decided that more action was needed. NCI's

---

36 Much of this section draws on two FTC staff reports: John E Calfee and Janis K Pappalardo (1989) *How Should Health Claims for Foods Be Regulated? An Economic Perspective*, Bureau of Economics, Federal Trade Commission, (September); and Pauline Ippolito and Alan Mathios (1989) *Health Claims in Advertising and Labeling: A Study of the Cereal Market*, Bureau of Economics Staff Report, Federal Trade Commission, (August).

cancer prevention division undertook to communicate the new information about fiber and cancer to the general public. Their goal was to change consumer diets and reduce the risk of cancer, but they had little hope of success given the tiny advertising budgets of agencies like NCI.

Their prospects unexpectedly brightened in 1984. NCI received a call from the Kellogg Corporation, whose All-Bran cereal held a commanding market share of the high fiber segment. Kellogg proposed to use All-Bran advertising as a vehicle for NCI's public service messages. NCI thought that was an excellent idea. Soon, an agreement was reached in which NCI would review Kellogg's ads and labels for accuracy and value before Kellogg began running their fiber-cancer ads.

The new Kellogg All-Bran campaign opened in October 1984. A typical ad began with the headline, '**At last some news about cancer you can live with.**' The ad continued,

> The National Cancer Institute believes a high fiber, low fat diet may reduce your risk of some kinds of cancer. The National Cancer Institute reports some very good health news. There is growing evidence that may link a high fiber, low fat diet to lower incidence of some kinds of cancer. That's why one of their strongest recommendations is to eat high fiber foods. If you compare, you'll find Kellogg's All-Bran has nine grams of fiber per serving. No other cereal has more. So start your day with a bowl of Kellogg's All-Bran or mix it with your regular cereal.

The ad included a graph comparing the Kellogg All-Bran's fiber content to that in other high fiber foods. It also provided NCI's address and toll-free telephone number for more information on cancer and fiber.

The Kellogg All-Bran campaign quickly achieved two things. One was to create a regulatory crisis between two agencies. The Food and Drug Administration thought that if a food was advertised as a way to prevent cancer, it was being marketed as a drug. Then the FDA's regulations for drug labeling would kick in. The food would be reclassified as a drug and would be removed from the market until the seller either stopped making the health claims or put the product through the clinical testing necessary to obtain formal approval as a drug.

But food advertising is regulated by the FTC, not the FDA. The FTC thought Kellogg's ads were non-deceptive and were therefore perfectly legal. In fact, the FTC thought the ads should be encouraged. The Director of the FTC's Bureau of Consumer Protection declared in a speech that 'the [Kellogg] ad has presented important public health recommendations in an accurate, useful and substantiated way. It informs the members of the public that there is a body of data suggesting certain relationships between cancer and diet that they may find important.' The FTC won this political battle, and the ads continued.[37]

The second instant effect of the All-Bran campaign was to unleash a flood of health claims. Vegetable oil manufacturers advertised that cholesterol was associated with coronary heart disease, and that vegetable oil does not contain cholesterol. Margarine ads did the same, and added that vitamin A is essential for good vision. Ads for calcium products (such as certain antacids) provided vivid demonstrations of the effects of osteoporosis (which weakens bones in old age), and recounted the advice of experts to increase dietary calcium as a way to prevent osteoporosis. Kellogg's competitors joined in citing the National Cancer Institute dietary recommendations. Oat bran cereals advertised the latest research on how dietary fiber can also reduce blood cholesterol and therefore, coronary heart disease.

Nor did things stop there. In the face of consumer demand for better and fuller information, health claims quickly evolved from a blunt tool to a surprisingly refined mechanism. Cereals were advertised as high in fiber *and* low in sugar or fat or sodium. Ads for an upscale brand of bread noted, 'Well, most high-fiber bran cereals may be high in fiber, but often only one kind: insoluble. It's this kind of fiber that helps promote regularity. But there's also a kind of fiber known as soluble, which most high-fiber bran cereals have in very small amounts, if at all. Yet diets high in this kind of fiber may actually lower your serum cholesterol, a risk factor for some heart diseases.' Cereal boxes became convenient sources for a summary of what made for a good diet.

---

37 The quotation is from 'Remarks of Carol T Crawford, Director of the Bureau of Consumer Protection, Federal Trade Commission, before the American Advertising Federation', 4 December 1984.

Non-government health groups also tried to play a role. Health claims in ads often suffered from lack of credibility. The Kellogg ads overcame this problem with the help of the National Cancer Institute. For claims about heart disease, an offer of help came from the American Heart Association, one of the pillars of the US public health community. The AHA announced a plan in which it would (for a fee) certify foods as part of a heart-healthy diet, and permit ads and labels to carry the AHA seal. FDA opposition eventually halted this plan, but it illustrates the potency of market forces for information. In fact, the idea has persisted. The AHA resurrected its plan in the mid-1990s, and the American Cancer Society announced a similar plan in 1997.

What was the effect of the health claims phenomenon that dominated food marketing in the second half of the 1980s? If it had amounted to nothing more than a steady flow of ads with tiny capsules of useful information about diet and health, that would have been remarkable enough. But the ads also brought powerful secondary effects. These may have been even more useful than the information that actually appeared in the ads themselves.

One effect was an increase in media coverage of diet and health. *Consumer Reports*, a venerable and hugely influential magazine that carries no advertising, revamped its reports on cereals to emphasize fiber and other ingredients (rather than testing the foods to see how well they did at providing a complete diet for laboratory rats). The health claims phenomenon generated its own press coverage; *Consumer Reports* published articles like 'What Has All-Bran Wrought?' and 'The Fiber Furor.' These stories recounted the ads and the scientific information that prompted the ads, and articles on food and health proliferated. Anyone who lived through these years in the United States can probably remember the unending media attention to health claims and to diet and health generally.

Much of the information on diet and health was new. This was no coincidence. Firms were sponsoring research on their products in the hope of finding results that could provide a basis for persuasive advertising claims. Oat bran manufacturers, for example, funded research on the impact of soluble fiber on blood cholesterol. When the results came out 'wrong,' as they did in a 1990 study published with great fanfare in the *New England*

Journal of Medicine, the headline in *Advertising Age* was 'Oat Bran Popularity Hitting the Skids,' and it did indeed tumble. The manufacturers kept at the research, however, and eventually the best research supported the efficacy of oat bran in reducing cholesterol (even to the satisfaction of the FDA). Thus did pure advertising claims spill over to benefit the information environment at large.[38]

In the late 1980s, economists and consumer researchers began to study the health-claims-for-foods phenomenon. Their findings provided stunning documentation of the power of advertising to solve seemingly intractable information problems. After years of stable fiber content in breakfast cereals, the average new cereal in the years after the All-Bran campaign started had roughly twice the fiber of cereals introduced in the years leading up to 1984. Meanwhile, products such as granola, which had previously carried a reputation for health despite containing a lot of fat and a little fiber, suffered grievous losses in market share.[39]

The shift to higher fiber cereals encompassed brands that had never undertaken the effort necessary to construct believable ads about fiber and disease. Two consumer researchers at the Food and Drug Administration reviewed these data and concluded they were 'consistent with the successful educational impact of the Kellogg diet and health campaign: consumers seemed to be making an apparently thoughtful discrimination between high and low fiber cereals,' and that the increased market shares for high-fiber

---

38 See *Advertising Age*, 21 May 1990, p 3. In the 13 April 1992 issue of *Forbes Magazine*, an article entitled 'Pass the Sugar', noted that Common Sense Oat Bran, Oatbake and Kenmei Rice Bran together commanded less than .5% of the ready-to-eat cereal market, and explained, 'All were done in by a 1990 article in the *New England Journal of Medicine* that questioned the value of oat bran in fighting cholesterol.' By 1992, the tables had been turned as a careful meta-analysis of oat bran research documented a significant effect on cholesterol; see *University of California at Berkeley Wellness Letter*, September 1992, p 7, 'Oat bran: the last word (for now)'. The FDA finally approved a health claim for oat bran in 1997; see *New York Times*, 26 February 1997, 'Oat Bran and Soluble Fiber: The Debate Continues', by Marian Burros.

39 Two FTC economists produced a series of studies, beginning with the official report cited earlier: Ippolito and Mathios (1989), *op cit*. Also see Ippolito and Mathios (1991) 'Health Claims in Food Marketing: Evidence on Knowledge and Behavior in the Cereal Market', *Journal of Public Policy and Marketing*, vol.10, no 1 (Spring), pp 15–32

non-advertised products represented 'the clearest evidence of a successful consumer education campaign.'[40]

These changes were remarkable. It is not easy to pump up fiber without sacrificing taste. The temptation is to add fat and sodium to improve flavor. FTC studies showed that this did not happen. Newer, higher fiber cereals actually contained less fat and sodium than cereals introduced before health claims began. The changes even spread beyond cereals to breads (despite little in the way of health claims by bread manufacturers). This reflected the sweeping changes in consumer information in the wake of the explicit health claims. Faced with these changing consumer dietary preferences, a major supermarket chain (again, with the cooperation of the National Cancer Institute) even undertook the difficult task of communicating health information about products such as fresh fruits and vegetables, where brands are of little importance and of necessity, there is little brand advertising to carry health claims.[41]

Perhaps most dramatic were the changes in consumer awareness of diet and health. The FTC analysis of US government surveys showed that when consumers were asked about how they could prevent cancer through their diet, the percentage who mentioned fiber increased from 4% (before the 1979 Surgeon General's report on diet and health) to 8.5% in 1984 (after the Surgeon General's report but before the All-Bran campaign) to 32% in 1986 after a year and a half or so of health claims (the figure in 1988 was 28%). The demographics are also of interest. By far the greatest increases in awareness were among women (who do most of the grocery shopping) and the less educated: up from 0% for women without a high school education in 1984 to 31% for the same group in 1986. For women with incomes of less than $15,000, the increase was from 6% to 28%.[42]

The health claims advertising phenomenon achieved what years of effort by government agencies had failed to achieve. With its mastery of the art of brevity, its ability to command attention, and its use of television,

---

40 The FDA study was Alan Levy and Raymond C Stokes (1987) 'Effects of a Health Promotion Advertising Campaign on Sale of Ready-to-Eat Cereals', 102 *Public Health Record* No 4 (July–August), pp 398–403.

41 Calfee and Pappalardo (1989), *op cit*.

42 Ippolito and Mathios (1989), *op cit*, and Ippolito and Mathios (1991), *op cit*.

brand advertising touched precisely the people the public health community was most desperate to reach. The health claims expanded consumer information along a broad front. The benefits clearly extended far beyond the interests of the relatively few manufacturers who made vigorous use of health claims in advertising.[43]

Beyond Health Claims for Foods

If I have devoted inordinate space to health claims for foods, it is because their controversial nature made them one of the most thoroughly examined episodes ever seen in the dynamics of advertising and information. They are only one example, however, of a pervasive phenomenon – the use of advertising to provide essential health information with benefits extending beyond the interests of the advertisers themselves. Other examples are worth exploring briefly.

Advertising for soap and detergents once improved private hygiene and therefore, public health (hygiene being one of the under-appreciated triumphs in twentieth century public health). Toothpaste advertising helped to do the same for teeth. When mass advertising for toothpaste and tooth powder began early in this century, toothbrushing was rare. It was common by the 1930s, after which toothpaste sales leveled off even though the advertising, of course, continued. When fluoride toothpastes became available, toothpaste manufacturers and the American Dental Association worked together (another example of market-driven 'certification' to achieve credibility) to generate interest in better teeth and professional dental care. Later, a 'plaque reduction war' (which first involved mouthwashes, and later toothpastes) brought a new awareness of gum disease and how to prevent it. The financial gains to the toothpaste industry were surely dwarfed by the benefits to consumers in the form of fewer cavities and fewer lost teeth.[44]

---

43 In addition to the work already cited, see the appropriately titled article by V S Freimuth, S L Hammond, and J A Stein (1988) 'Health Advertising: Prevention for Profit', 78 *American Journal of Public Health*, pp 557–561

44 Dentifrice advertising and its apparent effects are discussed in Borden (1942), *op cit*, pp 294–300. The beneficial effects of the ADA's endorsement of Crest toothpaste is well-known. On the 'plaque war', which was induced by ads for Listerine mouthwash and a little-known toothpaste brand, see 'Toothpastes', *Consumer Reports*, March 1986, and *Newsweek*, 28 October 1985, p 76, where Dr Irwin D Mandel, director of the Center for Clinical Research in Dentistry at Columbia University, is quoted as saying, 'All this attention [to plaque reduction] is good; it creates an atmosphere where people pay more attention to oral hygiene.'

One of the most noticed US television ads in recent years was the one with an elderly woman lying on the floor of her apartment and crying, 'Help! I've fallen and I can't get up.' This ad provoked unending satire (my favorite is the T-shirt that says 'help, I've dropped my remote control and I'm too lazy to pick it up.') But here is what the April 1995 *Harvard Health Letter* said of the ad and its signature line, 'This notorious phrase from a 1990 television commercial for 'panic button' devices created a fallout of jokes, T-shirts, and fodder for late-night comedians. It also transformed the sleepy market for personal response emergency systems (PERS) into a booming business. Although the ads were ridiculed by many, they dealt with a topic that is deadly serious.' Again, a small financial return to the advertisers probably brought much larger benefits in terms of the health and safety of the elderly.

Now consider the case of TPA, a new biotechnology drug that dissolves blood clots. Clinical trials recently demonstrated that TPA can do what no other medical treatment has ever been able to do: reverse the effects of a major stroke. Physicians have described their amazement at seeing patients arrive at the hospital unable to speak and leave a few hours later in full control of their capacities. For TPA to work, however, patients must reach a hospital emergency room within an hour or so of the stroke, and treatment must be prompt. The headline for an American Medical Association news release summed up the new situation: 'New Drug for Stroke Only as Good as Systems That Go Along with It: changes in healthcare systems and education of general public are key.' In other words, the drug would not do a lot of good without a revolution in how strokes are recognized and treated.[45]

The AMA's call for change reflected the state of medical practice. Until the advent of TPA, strokes (even serious ones) did not require quick transportation to a hospital for prompt treatment. Even the most skilled physician could do little beyond providing comfort followed by hopeful waiting. Now, all is different. Potential stroke victims and their families have to recognize the signs of a stroke so they can seek immediate treatment. Emergency telephone services ('911' in the US, '999' in the UK) and

---

45 See the 29 January 1997 edition of the AMA's 'Science News Update', released shortly after the FDA approved TPA for strokes.

ambulance personnel must recognize when a stroke has occurred and, contrary to years of training, seek the quickest possible treatment. Emergency room personnel must have the equipment and know-how to perform the necessary diagnostics (including CAT-scans) and administer TPA when necessary. Even family and emergency physicians have a lot to learn, as is evident from reports from the American Medical Association.[46]

As the American Medical Association and others have pointed out, what is needed is a major re-education campaign. Guess who has taken the lead? Within months after the FDA approved TPA for treating strokes, the manufacturer (Genentech) ran full-page ads in major newspapers with the headline, '425,000 strokes are uncalled for,' followed by a concise explanation of strokes and what to do to get help. Genentech is also funding conferences and training for medical personnel – and again, placing ads, in this case full-page ads in the *Journal of the American Medical Association.* The drug is expensive (roughly $2,000 per treatment according to recent reports) but untreated strokes are even more expensive. The remarkable benefits covered by the high price include not only the promise of saving lives but also an immense and costly change in the information environment.[47]

The necessity for re-education about strokes is part of a larger phenomenon. The public may be missing out on numerous valuable medical treatments purely because of inadequate dissemination of new information. Physicians groups have recently urged action to address the undertreatment of other dangerous conditions, including depression, hypertension and elevated cholesterol.[48] Again, it is the manufacturers of

---

46 See the following stories in the AMA's 'Science News Update' for the week of 29 January 1997: 'Most Hospitals Lack Acute Stroke Treatment Protocols: Detroit hospital model for acute treatment of stroke', and 'Primary Care Physicians Hold a Key in Battle Against Stroke: Timing and education make a difference'.

47 The headline is from the 2 May 1997 *New York Times*. A different ad with the same headline ran in the 28 May 1997 issue of *JAMA*. Also see the AMA's 'Science News Update' for 29 January 1997: 'TPA Significantly Reduces Costs for Appropriate Stroke Patients: Stroke costs US $30 billion annually; quick treatment key to lowering expenses, complications'.

48 See American Medical Association (1977) 'Science News Update' for the week of 29 January 1997, 'Depression Seriously Undertreated'.

the drugs that treat these conditions who have undertaken advertising to alert consumers to the possibility of dealing with conditions that either are without symptoms (high cholesterol) or are often assumed to be beyond medical treatment (depression).[49]

A truly remarkable episode now unfolding in the United States is the advertising battle among the various 'statin' drugs, a new generation of cholesterol-reducing medications. These drugs are the first to provide reliable reductions in cholesterol without serious side effects. The opportunity to market these drugs to millions of severely and mildly hypercholesterolemic patients generated a series of expensive clinical trials on the effects of cholesterol reduction on heart attacks and mortality. These trials yielded spectacular results and for the first time demonstrated the validity of the long-held, but unproven, proposition that reducing blood cholesterol would reduce deaths.[50]

Now competing manufacturers of cholesterol-reducing statin drugs are educating both physicians and consumers about the importance of cholesterol and the life-saving prospects offered by the new therapies. The battle is over the type of supporting evidence (not all have conducted trials involving mortality, for example), side effects, and patient compliance with medication (always a problem with an illness that has no symptoms). Some typical claims are: 'the buildup of evidence: epidemiologic investigations have established that cardiovascular morbidity and mortality are correlated with the level of cholesterol;' 'only Pravachol is proven to reduce the risk of *first MI* [myocardial infarction, or heart attack] by 31%;' 'any statin can say it lowers cholesterol; only Zocor has been proven to save lives.'[51] Those were taken from medical journals, but many of the same

---

48 See American Medical Association (1997) 'Science News Update' for the week of 29 January 1997, 'Depression Seriously Undertreated'.

49 For example, ads for BuSpar, a non-habitforming anti-anxiety drug, have described the connections between anxiety, a condition often misdiagnosed by consumers and physicians alike, and general well-being. The point of the ads, of course, is that many families are suffering from a treatable condition. The associated web site is: www.anxiety-relief.com, run by the manufacturer, Bristol-Myers Squibb.

50 See Martijn B Katan (8 May 1997) 'Review of D John Betteridge, ed, *Lipids: Current Perspectives'*, 336/19 *New England Journal of Medicine*, p 1394.

51 Ads for Lipitor and Pravachol (15 May 1997) and Zocor (7 August 1997) respectively in the *New England Journal of Medicine*.

manufacturers are also running full-page newspaper and magazine ads with similar messages about the relationship between cholesterol and heart attacks. These multi-million dollar campaigns are doing much to reduce the information deficit deplored by the American Medical Association and others.

Practical Lessons in Advertising and Information

These episodes in health advertising and information yield three paramount lessons. First, brand advertising can fill in holes in consumer information. It provides information that is of broad value to consumers yet is not furnished by traditional sources of information (at least not until advertising provokes the news media to expand coverage). Once unleashed from its regulatory prison, competitive advertising of health claims for foods proved to be pervasive, relentless (ask anyone in the packaged food business about this) and surprisingly extensive in its effects on information. Health claims induced changes in foods, in non-foods such as toothpaste, in publications ranging from *Consumer Reports* and university health letters to mainstream newspapers and magazines, and of course, consumer knowledge of diet and health.

These rippling effects from health claims in ads demonstrated the most basic propositions in the economics of information. Useful information initially failed to reach people who needed it because information producers could not charge a price to cover the costs of creating and disseminating pure information. And, this problem was alleviated by advertising, sometimes in a most vivid manner.

Other examples of spillover benefits from advertising are far more common than most people realize. Even the much-maligned promotion of expensive new drugs can bring profound health benefits to patients and families, far exceeding what is actually charged for the products themselves.

The second lesson is that the market processes that produce these benefits bear all the classic features of competitive advertising. We are not analyzing 'public service announcements' or public-spirited good-will ads, but old-fashioned profit-seeking brand advertising. Sellers focused on the information that favored their own products. They advertised it in ways that provided a close link between health benefits and their own brand.

Their advertising spit out information in small bits and pieces, and the core messages proceeded incrementally from topic to topic (from fiber to soluble fiber to fat and sugar and sodium, from cancer to blood cholesterol to heart disease). Advertisers tried to free-ride on their competitors ('oat bran for health,' and the like, without supporting detail). Sellers parlayed research results to their advantage when they could, and they suffered when the research turned out unfavorably. It was a purely competitive enterprise, and (as in Adam Smith's famous 'invisible hand') the benefits to consumers arose from the imperatives of the competitive process.[52]

The third lesson is simple: excessive regulation of advertising is a threat to information and sometimes, to public health. It took a courageous FTC and a stubbornly public-spirited National Cancer Institute to stage a public battle with NCI's powerful sister agency, the FDA. It is utterly clear from the FDA's history and subsequent behavior, incidentally, that the FDA would never have permitted any of these health claims in the absence of intense outside pressure. This is the agency that in the 1960s sought to stop food manufacturers from even mentioning 'cholesterol' or 'saturated fat' in ads or labels, and threatened litigation against any firm that dared to repeat the advice of public health groups to prevent heart disease by reducing dietary fat and cholesterol. It is no coincidence that the firm that broke the regulatory barriers to health claims for foods was Kellogg, which had no products under FDA review and therefore had no fear of the FDA's legendary ability to stifle not only advertising and marketing but even public criticism of the agency's policies.[53]

---

52 'Every individual… endeavors as much as he can… to direct industry so that its produce is of the greatest value … He generally, indeed, neither intends to promote the public interest, nor knows how much he is promoting it… [H]e intends only his own gain, and he is in this, as in many other cases, led by an invisible hand to promote an end which was no part of his intention. Nor is it always the worse for society that it was no part of it. By pursuing his own interest he frequently promotes that of the society more effectually than when he really intends to promote it. I have never known much good done by those who affected to trade for the public good.' Adam Smith, *The Wealth of Nations*, reprinted in part in Robert L Heilbroner, ed (1986) *The Essential Adam Smith*, W W Norton & Co, p 265.

53 On the peculiar institutional setting of FDA regulation of advertising, and the consequent ability of the FDA to impose advertising restrictions on pharmaceutical firms without regard to normal legal restraints, see my article, 'The Leverage Principle in FDA Regulation of Information', in Robert Helms, ed (1996) *Competitive Strategies in the Pharmaceutical Industry*, Washington, DC: American Enterprise Institute, pp 306–321

Now that the FDA again has direct influence on health claims for foods (through legislation passed in 1990), it is again in a position to prevent useful health advertising. As the FTC staff have themselves pointed out in public comments and articles, the FDA has implemented its new powers by greatly restricting the number of permitted health claims and, equally important, by requiring that health claims be made in a format that requires sellers to make their claims for entire product categories instead of one brand.[54]

These regulations have greatly limited health claims on labels and in ads because the FTC, which regulates ads, is now reluctant to permit claims not endorsed by the FDA.[55] A notable example occurred in 1992 when another federal agency, the Center for Disease Control, issued a recommendation that women of child-bearing age take folic acid supplements in order to prevent spina bifida, a severe birth defect. The recommendation was based on epidemiological research showing that folic acid reduced the incidence of these birth defects by half. Nevertheless, the FDA immediately announced it would prosecute any food or vitamin supplements manufacturer who mentioned the CDC recommendation in their labeling.[56] This removed virtually all financial incentive to disseminate this information to women. Two years later, it was obvious that folic acid intake was still far below the recommended level despite the CDC's advice.[57] The FDA finally issued a formal rule permitting a health claim for folic acid and birth defects on March 5, 1996, although by then legislation had placed supplements claims beyond the FDA's reach.

54 See Pauline Ippolito and Alan Mathios (1993) 'New Food Regulations and the Flow of Nutrition Information to Consumers', 12/2 *Journal of Public Policy and Marketing*, pp 188–205.

55 See *Los Angeles Times*, 8 May 1995, p B6, 'It's Good For You – But Don't Expect Labels to Say That', by Denise Gellene. The article notes, 'The lack of boastfulness among food producers [about health benefits of fiber, calcium, etc.] is one of the unexpected results of federal food labeling reforms, which are a year old today.'

56 *Boston Globe*, 17 Sept 1992, p 3, 'FDA Issues a Caveat to Advice on Folic Acid.' The article said, 'Within hours after the US Public Health Service told women of child-bearing age to consumer 0.4 milligrams daily of folic acid, Dr David Kessler ... issued this caution ... "A link between folic acid and neural tube defects does not say that the FDA is ready to permit a health claim for folic acid." '

57 See *New York Times*, 4 March 1995, p 7, 'Advice Unheeded on Averting Birth Defects', by Gina Kolata, describing an article in the 17 May 1995 issue of the *Journal of the American Medical Association*, which described data from the years 1992–1994.

Of course, food is not the only area where over-regulation can impede advertising from solving information problems. Advertising of prescription drugs directly to consumers is illegal in virtually every developed nation except the US, where the rules are highly restrictive but not prohibitive. This prohibition is exceedingly unfortunate for consumers around the world. Much of the most useful advertising on health involves prescription drugs, including drugs to reduce cholesterol and to treat allergies, strokes and heart attacks. These are areas where traditional prohibitions on prescription drug advertising are having regrettable consequences for consumers. The usually repressive advertising regulators at the FDA should be commended for their unique willingness to countenance even a measure of direct-to-consumer advertising of prescription drugs.[58] In August 1997, the FDA announced new rules that make it feasible (albeit clumsy) to advertise prescription drugs on television in a fairly straightforward manner. Previous rules required that ads omit either the brand or the illness being treated, leaving viewers mystified by most ads.[59]

One might see all this as simply an extended example of the economics of information and greed. And indeed it is, if by greed one means the effort to earn a profit by providing what people are willing to pay for, even if what they want most is information rather than a tangible product. Selling cereal by telling people about the latest research on diet and cancer is a lot like selling newspapers by telling consumers about essential political developments. The point is that there is overwhelming evidence that unregulated economic forces dictate that much useful information will be provided by brand advertising, and *only* by brand advertising.

Of course, there is much more to the story. There is the question of how competition does the good I have described without doing even more harm elsewhere. After all, firms want to tell people only what is good about their brands, and people often want to know what is wrong with the brands. It turns out that competition takes care of this problem, too; see chapter 3.

---

58 On the potential benefits of direct-to-consumer advertising of prescription drugs, see Alison Masson and Paul Rubin (1985) 'Matching Prescription Drugs and Consumers: The Benefits of Direct Advertising', 313 *New England Journal of Medicine*, pp 513–515.

59 *Washington Post*, 9 August 1997, 'FDA Relaxes Rules for On-Air Drug Ads', by John Schwartz.

Before looking at the peculiar dynamics of competitive advertising, an even more fundamental issue requires attention. It is one thing to say that advertisers will provide useful information to consumers. It is quite another to say that consumers will believe what the ads say, or that advertisers will deserve to be believed. The key is overcoming consumer skepticism.

Consumer Skepticism – the 70% Majority and its Influence on Advertising

The typical consumer seems to feel this way about advertising: It is definitely informative and is the best means of learning what is in the market… But it is not as trustworthy as it should be for more often than not it fools the public and it is a fertile field for the operation of quacks… There are far too many fake testimonials… Too much money is spent for advertising – and yet buying by advertisements helps to save much money… There is no adequate equivalent for advertising – certainly it shouldn't be replaced by daily government bulletins – but it should be controlled and regulated by the government so that it may become more trustworthy.[60]

The lesson from health claims for foods and thousands of other advertising campaigns is that advertising can provide essential information that would otherwise be missing from markets. This much is ensured by the peculiar economic properties of information, particularly the inability to copyright pure information. But the story is not merely one of seller incentives. The will to persuade through information does not operate unopposed. It is confronted by the stubbornly skeptical consumer.

In the 1930s, when dictatorships stalked Europe and capitalism was under siege in the most capitalist nation on earth, the advertising trade quite naturally found itself in a crisis of confidence. The editors of *Sales Management,* one of the leading American trade publications of that era, commissioned a series of consumer surveys about advertising. This was in the early days of scientific polling, and as far as I can tell, little if any systematic data were then available on how consumers felt about

60 *Sales Management,* 'Attitude Test Shows Women and Old People Favor Advertising Most', 1 January 1936.

advertising. The *Sales Management* surveys apparently provided the first valid nationwide data on attitudes toward advertising.[61]

The findings were summed up in the quotation at the top of this section. The surveys revealed a paradox. People did not believe what advertising said, but they used it all the time to get information.

Was this a fluke of the times, a passing sentiment that reflected only the peculiar situation of the Depression era of the 1930s? Not at all. Survey researchers returned to the same topic in the 1950s and have never left it since. Some of the best research was done in the 1970s and 1980s, when identical questions were repeated over a decade or more. These surveys asked consumers whether they agree with various statements: 'most advertising is believable' (about 33% agreed, during 1971 through 1979), '… ads usually present a true picture' (20% agreed), 'ads are reliable sources of information' (only 16%), and 'business hoodwinks through advertising' (70% agreed with that stunner, during 1975–1987).

When these surveys asked whether consumers agreed with a positive statement about advertising's value as a source of information – 'advertising provides useful information about products and services' – nearly 80% agreed (this was for the years during 1974–1989). This, too, is an old attitude. A 1935 survey found that 76% agreed that 'without advertising the consumer would be seriously handicapped in shopping,' and 71%, that 'most retail store advertising is a valuable help in educating the consumer.' Other questions asked in the late 1930s induced largely similar results.

The basic findings are amazingly consistent. During the 1930s, when capitalism itself was under siege, during the 1970s, when anti-advertising sentiment produced vast new regulations for advertising, and during the 1980s when the Reagan administration largely retreated from the activism of the 1970s, the results were always the same. The great majority of consumers – about 70% on average – think that as a general rule, advertising claims cannot be believed. About the same proportion –

---

61 This section draws on John E Calfee and Debra Jones Ringold (1994) 'The Seventy Percent Majority: Enduring Consumer Beliefs About Advertising', *Journal of Public Policy and Marketing*, Vol.13, no 2 (Fall), pp 228-238.

another 70% majority – think advertising is a useful source of information. When surveys reach further, asking whether advertising 'encourages people to use products they don't need,' or whether 'advertising encourages people to use some products that are bad for them,' again, about 70% agree. And when consumers are asked whether there should be *more* regulation, there is, again, about a 70% agreement that, yes, stricter regulation is needed.

There is something else even more remarkable about the 70% majority. It seems to have populated the entire world. In a 1991 Canadian survey, 76% agreed that 'advertising is often misleading,' 77% agreed that 'advertising provides information that helps make a purchase decision,' and 68%, that 'advertising should be more tightly regulated.' [62]

A July 14, 1995 *Wall Street Journal* story carrying the headline 'Consumers Say They Aren't Buying Advertisers' Hard Sell, Survey Finds' described a Roper Starch survey of 38,000 consumers in 40 countries. The survey '…found 73% of consumers believe advertisers regularly mislead or exaggerate a product's benefits.' The article concluded with the quote at the beginning of this chapter: '…it's clear that despite all the billions advertisers spend to sway viewers and readers to buy their products, consumers are, at the very least, skeptical.'

Nor is this sentiment restricted to thoroughly westernized economies. The same survey found that 'consumers from the former Soviet Union proved to be the most leery of advertising. Only 9% of Russian and Ukrainian consumers felt advertising provided good, accurate information while just 10% said they felt advertisers respected their intelligence.' The article pointed out that those consumers had long been accustomed to dealing with advertising in the form of state propaganda rather than commercial advertising. That would explain such an extreme level of skepticism.

Clearly, we are dealing with some fundamental constants in consumer behavior. I can predict with considerable confidence that if someone were

---

62 F G Crane (1991) 'Consumers' Attitudes Towards Advertising: A Canadian Perspective', 10/2 *International Journal of Advertising*, pp 111–116.

to conduct a random survey tomorrow, it would reveal that most people (probably about 70%) think that they cannot believe most of what they see in advertising. And, what is almost as significant, pollsters and commentators and advertising industry leaders would immediately declare that advertising faced a credibility crisis. Various solutions would be proposed, probably including more or better self-regulation or government regulation. This happens over and over again. A December 16, 1991 *Advertising Age* story carried the headline, 'Poll: Ads strain credibility,' accompanied by a graph with the caption, 'Consumers don't believe Advertising: Seventy-five percent of respondents think all or some TV advertising is unbelievable.' That number was about the same as the one in the 1995 *Wall Street Journal* article cited above for its data on consumers around the world.

These numbers settle some questions and raise others. We can dismiss the idea that consumers are putty in the hands of advertisers. Consumers approach ads with skepticism. The starting point for consumer perceptions of advertising is something along the lines of a blanket assumption that advertising claims are unreliable unless there are concrete reasons for believing otherwise. If sellers are going to achieve anything through advertising, they are going to have to overcome that skepticism. How can they do that?

Beyond Consumer Skepticism – How Advertising Persuades

If no one believed anything they saw in ads, we wouldn't see much advertising because there wouldn't *be* much advertising. Why spend money to tell people what they won't believe? But advertising persists, including ads that contain a great deal of highly specific information (check this morning's newspaper). When so much money is spent by profit-seeking firms to give something to people, we can be sure that a lot of people use it. They are the second 70% majority, the one that thinks advertising is an essential source of information.

How can we resolve this apparent paradox in which consumers don't believe advertising but use it anyway? We need to think of sellers and consumers as participants in a continuous process. The process provides a way for ads to move from skepticism to persuasion. How so? One might guess that the key is the sheer force of repetition, the incessant hammering of claims that no one believes until, finally, many people believe. That, of course, is completely incorrect.

What makes information effective in advertising is to link it to yet more information – reliable sources, and especially, reliable brands. When the focus moves from advertising claims in the abstract to specific claims for specific brands sold at well-known retailers, much consumer skepticism disappears. Advertising for prices, for example, are treated almost with contempt when viewed abstractly ('how do I know what "one-half off the regular price" means?'). Attach the name of a familiar retailer and the claim gathers meaning. Consumers know whether a 'sale' is an everyday occurrence, or a rare one. Add brand names, and the ad means even more. Consumers have learned which brands to trust. Place all of this in a highly competitive, relatively unregulated environment – lots of price ads for familiar brands in familiar stores – and the seller faces a well-informed consumer who waits for ads that promise something not seen before (for instance, a better price on a carpet contemplated for the past year or two). Persuasion has emerged from skepticism.[63]

What happens is this: persuasion requires credibility. Credibility can be established, although with great difficulty. Then advertising can persuade. But credibility is easily lost. That is why oat bran sales plummeted in the wake of a single poorly designed study on oat bran and cholesterol.[64]

This is entirely a self-enforcing mechanism, driven by competition and the profit motive in the face of enduring consumer skepticism. When the FTC adopted its stringent new policies toward advertising claims in the 1970s, there was no visible effect on the overall level of consumer skepticism or on consumer approval of advertising as a source of information.

---

63 An old but still useful study is Joseph Fry and Gordon McDougall (1974) 'Consumer Appraisal of Retail Price Adjustments' 38 *Journal of Marketing*, pp 64–74. This study was an exception in that it used names of familiar retailers. Unfortunately, most research on the influence of price claims has been conducted through 'experiments' in which retailer and brand names are omitted or are irrelevant. See Dhruv Grewal and Larry D Compeau (1992) 'Comparative Price Advertising: Informative or Deceptive?' 11/1 *Journal of Public Policy and Marketing*, pp 52–66.

64 See the citations in the above section on health claims for foods.

The 70% majority had already arrived in the marketplace, and it remained unchanged through the years of regulatory expansion and continued in force through the deregulatory years of the 1980s. What makes advertising believable is not regulation, but the slow and painstaking efforts of sellers to establish reasons for people to believe their ads.

At this point, I think we can forget the idea that advertising exploits consumers. Consumers use advertising, and advertisers must adjust accordingly or risk failure. That leads to the next topic.

3 Advertising Under the Influence of Consumers and Competition

*'Takes the FEAR Out of Smoking' – 'Do you love a good smoke but not what the smoke does to you?' – 'takes out more nicotine and tars than any other leading cigarette – **the difference in protection is priceless'** [65]*

'Never before has an industry spent so much money trying to talk itself out of business. The 'commercials' keep reminding us that tobacco contains tars, resins, and other bronchial abrasives. Smokers are quite obviously committing slow suicide, but each brand claims that its own product is somewhat less lethal than other brands.' [66]

Consumers bring their knowledge and experience to bear on every ad they see. This experience is continually reshaped by information from thousands of sources, including advertising itself. Advertisers take this shifting environment into account and make changes of their own. The implication is straightforward but often overlooked. Individual ads are best understood as being a sort of freeze-frame from a long-running dialogue between sellers and consumers. Almost always, the meaning of what an advertisement says is profoundly shaped by what is happening elsewhere. To a much greater extent than most people realize, advertisers are pawns of the evolving information environment in which they must communicate. The failure to understand this has been a constant source of misconceptions about why advertising says what it says, how that information changes under the impact of information and competition, and most of all, how regulation works.

---

65 Ads for new filtertip cigarettes, 1953–54. The first ad was for Philip Morris, the last two for Kent. See John E Calfee, 'The Ghost of Cigarette Advertising Past', published in the November–December 1986 issue of *Regulation* magazine, and republished in the Summer 1997 issue of *Regulation*, Vol 20, No 3.

66 *Fortune* magazine, 'Embattled Tobacco's New Strategy', January 1963, p 100, quoting business commentator Herbert Leggett.

We can begin with the information in ads.

Bits and Pieces of Information – Advertising and Context

It is often said that most advertising does not contain very much information. In a way, this is true. Research on the contents of advertising typically finds just a few pieces of concrete information per ad. That's an average, of course. Some ads obviously contain a great deal of information. Still, a lot of ads are mainly images and pleasant talk, with little in the way of what most people would consider hard information. On the whole, information in advertising comes in tiny bits and pieces.

Cost is only one reason. To be sure, cramming more information into ads is expensive. But more to the point is the fact that advertising plays off the information available from outside sources. Hardly anything about advertising is more important than the interplay between what the ad contains and what surrounds it. Sometimes this interplay is a burden for the advertiser because it is beyond his control. But the interchange between advertising and environment is also an invaluable tool for sellers. Ads that work in collaboration with outside information can communicate far more than they ever could on their own.

The upshot is advertising's astonishing ability to communicate a great deal of information in a few words. Economy and vividness of expression almost always rely upon what is in the information environment. The famously concise 'Think Small' and 'Lemon' ads for the VW 'Beetle' in the 1960s and 1970s were highly effective with buyers concerned about fuel economy, repair costs and extravagant styling in American cars. This was a case where the less said, the better. The ads were more powerful when consumers were free to bring their own ideas about the issues at hand.[67]

The same process is repeated over again for all sorts of products. Ads for computer modems once explained what they could be used for. Now a simple reference to the Internet is sufficient to conjure an elaborate mix of equipment and applications. These matters are better left vague so

---

[67] This point is illustrated nicely in David Ogilvy's *Ogilvy on Advertising*, Vintage Books (1985), pp 13 and 73.

each potential customer can bring to the ad his own idea of what the Internet is really for.

Let us think about some of the consequences of the subtle interplay between sparse information in advertising and plentiful information in the surrounding environment. One result is pure efficiency in communication. This involves more than simply communicating cheaply. Economy in information also makes it easier to reach those consumers who are most likely to appreciate what the seller has to offer. For example, an East Coast US retailer uses the motto, 'the educated consumer is our best customer.' This retailer happens to specialize in 'off-price' (i.e., heavily discounted) women's clothes bearing prestigious brands. The motto refers to the fact that bargains are available for those who know their brands and styles. An ad containing a more thorough explanation would probably attract a different audience with different tastes. It could even miss the prime target and thereby defeat the purpose of operating this kind of outlet. Hence more 'informative' advertising can actually sacrifice some of the efficiencies gained through target marketing.

Leaning on information from other sources is also a way to enhance credibility, without which advertising must fail. Much of the most important information in advertising – think of cholesterol and heart disease, antilock brakes and automobile safety – acquires its force from highly credible sources *other* than the advertiser. To build up this kind of credibility through material actually contained in ads would be cumbersome and inefficient. Far more effective, and far more economical, is the technique of making challenges, raising questions and otherwise making it perfectly clear to the audience that the seller invites comparisons and welcomes the tough questions. Hence the classic slogan, 'If you can find a better whiskey, buy it.'

Finally, there is the most important point of all. Informational sparseness facilitates competition. It is easier to challenge a competitor through pungent slogans – 'Where's the beef?', 'Where's the big saving?' – than through a step-by-step recapitulation of what has gone on before. The bits-and-pieces approach makes for quick, unerring attacks and equally quick responses, all under the watchful eye of the consumer over whom the battle is being fought. This is an ideal recipe for competition.

It also brings the competitive market's fabled self-correcting forces into play. Sellers are less likely to stretch the truth, whether it involves prices or subtleties about safety and performance, when they know they may arouse a merciless response from injured competitors. That is one reason the FTC once worked to get comparative ads on television, and has sought for decades to dismantle government or voluntary bans on comparative ads. The FTC is taking advantage of the general rule that efficiency in communication begets efficiency in competition.

There is a troubling possibility, however. Is it not possible that in their selective and carefully calculated use of outside information, advertisers have the power to focus consumer attention exclusively on the positive, i.e., on what is good about the brand or even the entire product class? Won't automobile ads talk up style, comfort, and extra safety, while food ads do taste and convenience, cigarette ads do flavor and life-style, and airlines do comfort and frequency of departure, all the while leaving consumers to search through other sources to find all the things that are wrong with products?

In fact, this is not at all what happens. Here is why.

Products That Aren't Perfect: the Dynamics of 'Less Bad' Advertising

'**Cough** … the problem has been solved by … Glyco-Heroin… the Sum of Clinical Experience Designates Glyco-Heroin as a Respiratory Sedative superior in All Respects to the Preparations of Opium, Morphine, Codeine and Other Narcotics and withal devoid of the toxic or depressing effects which characterize the latter when given in doses sufficient to reduce the reflex irritability of the bronchial, tracheal and laryngeal mucous membranes.' [68]

Everything for sale has something wrong with it, if only the fact that you have to pay for it. Some products, of course, are notable for their faults.

---

68 From a turn-of-the-century ad for a new cough syrup, based on a newly discovered drug which the Bayer company had named 'heroin,' shortly before it invented the name 'aspirin' for another amazing new drug. This ad is reproduced in color in David Must's fascinating article, 'Opium, Cocaine and Marijuana in American History, *Scientific American*, July 1991, pp 40–47.

The most obvious examples involve tobacco and health, but there is also food and heart disease, drugs and side effects, vacations and bad weather, automobiles and accidents, airlines and delay, among others. Believe it or not, the quotation above is exactly what a close reading suggests. It was from a heroin ad based on the argument that heroin was not as bad as opium, morphine and other competing cough medicines (all legal at the time, of course).

Products and their problems bring into play one of the most important ways in which the competitive market induces sellers to serve the interests of buyers. No matter what the product, there are usually a few brands that are 'less bad' than the others. The natural impulse is to advertise that advantage – 'less cholesterol,' 'less fat,' 'less dangerous,' and so on. Such provocative claims tend to have an immediate impact. The targets often retaliate; maybe their brands are less bad in a different respect (less salt?). The ensuing struggle brings better information, more informed choices and improved products.

We can begin with perhaps the most riveting episode of 'less-bad' advertising ever seen. It occurred, amazingly enough, in the industry that most people assume is the master of *avoiding* saying anything bad about their product. If less-bad advertising can work in this market, it can work in any market. The market in question is, of course, tobacco.

Cigarette advertising was once very different from what it is today. Cigarettes first became popular around the time of World War I, and they came to dominate the tobacco market in the 1920s. Steady and often dramatic sales increases continued into the 1950s, always with vigorous support from advertising. Tobacco advertising was duly celebrated as an outstanding example of the power and creativity of advertising. Yet amazingly, much of the advertising focussed on what was *wrong* with smoking, rather than what people liked about smoking.[69]

69 This section draws on my work on cigarette advertising, especially 'The Ghost of Cigarette Advertising Past', *op cit*; 'Cigarette Advertising, Health Information and Regulation Before 1970', released in December 1985 as Working Paper #134 by the Bureau of Economics in the Federal Trade Commission (and also available from the author at the American Enterprise Institute); and 'The Informational Content of Cigarette Advertising: 1926–86', (written with Debra Ringold), *Journal of Public Policy and Marketing*, vol 8 (1989), pp 1–23. Those articles, especially the FTC working paper, supply extensive documentation, including citations for many of the items presented here without supporting citation.

The very first ad for the very first mass-marketed American cigarette brand (Camel, the same brand recently under attack for its use of a cartoon character) said, 'Camel Cigarettes *will not* sting the tongue and *will not* parch the throat.' When Old Gold broke into the market in the mid-1920s, it did so with an ad campaign about coughs and throats and harsh cigarette smoke. It settled on the slogan, 'not a cough in a carload' even as critics in the advertising trade argued, '[T]his form of advertising was not well conceived ... To convey to the cigarette smoker directly or indirectly the idea of any harmful or unpleasant effects from cigarette smoking cannot be considered good policy either from the standpoint of the industry generally or eventually of the manufacturer who advertises it.' [70]

Nonetheless, competitors responded in kind. Soon, advertising left no doubt about what was wrong with smoking. Lucky Strike ads said, 'No Throat Irritation – No Cough ... we ... removed ... harmful corrosive acids,' and later on, 'Do you inhale? What's there to be afraid of? ... famous purifying process removes certain impurities.' Camel's famous tag line, 'more doctors smoke Camels than any other brand,' carried a punch precisely because many authorities thought smoking was unhealthy (cigarettes were called 'coffin nails' back then), and smokers were eager for reassurance in the form of smoking by doctors themselves. This particular ad, which was based on surveys of physicians, ran in one form or another from 1933 to 1955. It achieved prominence partly because physicians practically never endorsed non-therapeutic products. The ad ran in many outlets including the *Journal of the American Medical Association*, which regularly carried cigarette advertisements until the early 1950s. Incidentally, Camel was by no means the only brand that cited medical authorities in an effort to reassure smokers.[71]

When *Readers Digest* (which often carried articles on the dangers of smoking) published a report in 1942 on the tar content of cigarette smoke,

---

70 The Camel ad is reproduced in *How It Was In Advertising: 1776–1976*, compiled by the editors of *Advertising Age*, Chicago: Crain Books, 1976. Also see R T Hanley (1927) 'An Entire Industry Turns to Negative Advertising: Explaining How the Cigarette Business Developed a Coughing Spell', *Printers Ink*, (19 December), p 10.

71 See Alan Blum's highly informative article, 'When "More Doctors Smoked Camels" Cigarette Advertising in the *Journal*', 83 *New York State Journal of Medicine*, no 13 (December 1983), pp 1347–1352.

Old Gold ads actually urged smokers to *read* the article. That article said Old Gold cigarettes contained less tar than other leading brands, but then it went on to say that the differences were so small that 'the smoker … need no longer worry as to which cigarette can most effectively nail down his coffin. For one nail is just about as good as another.' The FTC sued Old Gold's manufacturer because its ads did not mention that last remark.

Things really got interesting in the early 1950s, when the first persuasive medical reports on smoking and lung cancer reached the public. These reports created a phenomenal stir among smokers and the public generally. People who do not understand how advertising works would probably assume that cigarette manufacturers used advertising to divert attention away from the cancer reports. In fact, they did the opposite.

Small brands could not resist the temptation to use advertising to scare smokers into switching brands. They inaugurated several spectacular years of 'fear advertising' that sought to gain competitive advantage by exploiting smokers' new fear of cancer. Lorillard, the beleaguered seller of Old Gold, introduced Kent, a new filter brand supported by ad claims like these: 'sensitive smokers get real health protection with new Kent,' 'Do you love a good smoke but not what the smoke does to you?,' and 'takes out more nicotine and tars than any other leading cigarette – *the difference in protection is priceless,'* illustrated by television ads showing the black tar trapped by Kent's filters.

Other manufacturers came out with their own filter brands, and raised the stakes with claims like, 'NOSE, THROAT, and Accessory Organs not Adversely Affected by Smoking Chesterfields. First Such Report Ever Published About Any Cigarette,' 'Takes the Fear Out of Smoking,' and 'Stop worrying … Philip Morris and only Philip Morris is *entirely free* of irritation used [sic] in *all other* leading cigarettes.'

Observers were astonished at these ads and their obvious impact on smokers. *Consumer Reports* magazine noted in February 1953 that, '… smokers are often aware that cigarette smoking may not be good for them and they don't like to be reminded of it by [health themes in] ads… Ads claiming health advantages for a particular brand merely underscore the possible dangers from smoking, to the detriment of the whole industry …' Practically everyone who looked at the cigarette market during those years arrived at the same conclusion. For example, a prominent medical journalist wrote in 1954, 'the net result [of recent advertising about effects of smoking] was to set the impressionable smoker to wondering whether it was safe even to carry a cigarette in his pocket.' A 1963 book on the history of advertising similarly concluded that 'the tobacco companies, aware of the alarm among cigarette smokers, had worked themselves into a corner in their ads and were, in effect, promoting brands on a my-brand-gives-less-cancer-than-your-brand basis.' [72]

These ads threatened to demolish the industry. As 'bitter words were hurled by tobacco growers who accused cigarette advertisers of fouling the common nest,' cigarette sales plummeted by 3% in 1953 and a remarkable 6% in 1954. Never again, not even in the face of the most impassioned anti-smoking publicity by the US Surgeon General or the Food and Drug Administration, would cigarette consumption decline as rapidly as it did during these years of entirely market-driven anti-smoking ad claims by the cigarette industry itself. *Business Week* noted, 'there is no question but that the tobacco companies themselves have helped cause the sales drop... [The advertising] scared some smokers out of the cigarette habit by claiming that each brand of cigarette does not contain the harmful ingredients [that others contain].' [73]

Thus advertising traveled full circle. Devised to bolster brands, it denigrated the product so much that overall market demand actually declined. Everyone understood what was happening, but the fear ads continued because they helped the brands that used them.[74] The new filter

---

72 The medical journalist was Bob Considine, quoted from his article, 'To Smoke Or Not To Smoke', published in April 1954 in a *Cosmopolitan* magazine that was very different from the one we know today. Also see Joseph J Seldin (1963) *The Golden Fleece: Selling the Good Life to Americans*, (out of print), p 122. Here is a sample of similar readings of the events of the early 1950s: *The Consumers Union Report on Smoking and the Public Interest*, New York, 1963; *Business Week*, 'Cigarette Scare: What'll the Trade Do?', 5 December 1953, p 68; *Consumer Reports*, February 1955, pp 56–73; *Fortune* magazine 'The Uproar in Cigarettes', December 1953, p 130, and 'Embattled Tobacco's ...', 1963, *op cit*; and *The New Republic*, 7 May 1966, p 7.

73 The quote about tobacco growers is from Roy Norr, 'Now Everybody's Getting Scared', originally published in the *Christian Herald* in January 1954 and reprinted in 'False and Misleading Advertising (Filter-tip Cigarettes)', Hearings before a Subcommittee of the Committee on Government Operations, House of Representatives, 85th Cong., 1st Sess., 18–26 July 1957, pp 743–746. *The Business Week* quote is from 21 November 1953, p 145.

74 *Business Week*, 19 June 1954, p 58, noted that fear ads 'may boost an individual brand's share of the market, but what good is that if the whole market dwindles?'.

brands (all from smaller manufacturers) gained a foothold even as their ads amplified the medical reports on the dangers of smoking.

The cigarette market in the early 1950s provided what should have been an unforgettable lesson in how competitive advertising serves the consumer interest even in situations where almost everyone would assume it serves only the industry. On the whole, cigarette advertising probably raised stronger alarms about the health effects of smoking than medical experts did. Neither the federal government nor public health groups such as the American Medical Association and the American Cancer Society were campaigning against smoking. In fact, they were trying to reassure smokers that the evidence linking smoking and cancer was very preliminary and that there was no reason to quit smoking. Nonetheless, sales plummeted.

The contrast with later years is instructive. In 1957-1959 and again in 1963-1964, far more compelling medical news about smoking and cancer would arrive. Neither episode had an impact on cigarette sales comparable to the events of 1950-1953. But by 1957, as we shall see, cigarette advertising had been cleaned up by the FTC so that overt fear advertising was no longer a factor.[75]

It was only after the FTC stopped the fear ads in 1955 (on the grounds that the implied health claims had no proof) that sales resumed their customary annual increases. No wonder the advertising trade magazine *Printers Ink* declared in its annual review of cigarette advertising,

> The saga of cigarette advertising for 1955 filters came down to this: *Good taste took over.* Advertising copy stressed good taste, flavor and enjoyment consistently. Ads themselves, on the whole, seemed in better taste. By and large, whatever grim messages remained from the health scare days gave way to pleasant, almost 'Pollyanna' prose.[76]

In other words, the regulators forced the industry to stop shooting itself in the foot. Although this episode is forgotten today, it was understood

---

75 The February 1954 issue of *Consumer Reports* relayed the following advice from its board of medical advisors: 'Until proof is forthcoming, it is obvious that those who can should cut their smoking to what is considered moderate levels – certainly not more than a pack a day.' The events of 1957-59 and 1963-64 are recounted in Carl Scheraga and John E Calfee (1996) 'The Industry Effects of Information and Regulation In the Cigarette Market: 1950-1965,' 15 *Journal of Public Policy and Marketing*, pp 216-226.

76 Emphasis in original; *Printer's Ink*, 30 December 1955, p 15.

perfectly by contemporary observers as diverse as *Business Week, Fortune, Consumer Reports* and even anti-tobacco advocates.

Fear advertising has never quite left the tobacco market despite the regulatory straightjacket that governs cigarette advertising. In 1957, when leading cancer experts advised smokers to ingest less tar, the industry responded by cutting tar and citing tar content figures compiled by independent sources. A stunning 'tar derby' reduced the tar and nicotine content of cigarettes by 40% in four years, a far more rapid decline than would be achieved by years of government urging in later decades.[77]

This episode, too, was halted by the FTC. In February 1960 the FTC engineered a 'voluntary' ban on tar and nicotine claims. Tobacco's fans at *Printers Ink* immediately grasped that this meant an end to almost everything the industry did not want to see in its own advertising:

> Completely erased, at the 'urging' of the Federal Trade Commission, are the boxscores on tar and nicotine. Once more the industry is back to its traditional and usually successful course – advertising flavor, taste and pleasure against a backdrop of beaches, ski slopes and languid lakes. It is a formula that works, as all-time high sales show in the Wootten Report.[78]

Consumer Reports, anything but a friend of tobacco, said much the same thing in its April 1961 issue: 'the cigarette industry had finally extricated itself from the embarrassing position it occupied for half a decade – that of constantly reminding its customers through its own advertising that the product it sold carried a threat to their health.'

Later research has indicated that when the FTC stopped fear advertising in 1955 and stopped the tar derby in 1960, stock prices in the tobacco industry recovered. This was especially true for the larger firms, who had avoided mentioning tar or fear and criticized those who did. Research on the effects of the 1970 ban on broadcast advertising reached

---

77 'Ghost of Cigarette Advertising Past', *op cit.*
78 'Cigarette Ads Back on Old Path', *Printer's Ink*, 23 December 1960, p 37.

similar conclusions in an article entitled, 'Finessing the Political System.'
That intriguing thought is explored further in chapter 5 on ad bans. [79]

More subtle fear advertising again became common in the 1970s with
phrases like, 'All the fuss about smoking got me thinking I'd either quit or
smoke True' and 'If it wasn't for Winston, I wouldn't smoke.' Another tar
derby ensued (tar and nicotine claims were permitted in 1966, and were
required in ads in 1970). Per capita sales turned downward and began a
slide from which the industry has yet to recover. In the 1980s, when
RJ Reynolds introduced a smokeless cigarette called Premier, it was widely
expected that RJR would promote Premier by appealing to smokers' fear of
the contents of cigarette smoke. Amazingly, this innovation encountered
intense hostility from anti-smoking advocates, but it failed anyway because
smokers did not like it. [80]

Further episodes continue to this day. In 1993, Liggett planned an
advertising campaign to emphasize that its Chesterfield brand did not use
the stems and other less desirable parts of the tobacco plant. This touched a
nerve. The *Wall Street Journal* noted that at a time when critics were pushing
for FDA regulation of cigarettes as a drug, 'Liggett's ad points out tactlessly
just how little puffers really know about what goes into their lungs.'
A Liggett marketing executive responded that large manufacturers have a
'vested interest in not telling. We, being the little guy, might as well tell the
truth and make hay with it.'

In 1994, RJR test-marketed a less pungent brand of menthol cigarette.
Advertising analysts promptly pointed out that '… it's a gamble to point out
negative features associated with smoking,' and added, 'saying that you are
making your product less bad can be a double-edged sword.' Barely a year
before this book was written, RJR test-marketed another smokeless cigarette
called Eclipse. Like Premier, its appeal derived from the fact that it emitted
no smoke and therefore, no tar. Eclipse immediately aroused criticism

---

79 Carl Scheraga and John E Calfee (1996) *op cit.* Mark Mitchell and H Harold Mulherin (1988)
    'Finessing the Political System: The Cigarette Advertising Ban', 54 *Southern Economic Journal*,
    pp 855–862.

80 *Washington Post*, Health Section, 6 September 1988, p 6.

within the industry because it blatantly suggested the need for 'safer' cigarettes.[81]

This continuing episode, extending through eight decades, is perhaps the best documented case of how 'less-bad' advertising completely offsets any desires by sellers to accentuate the positive while ignoring the negative. *Consumer Reports* magazine's 1955 assessment of the new fear of smoking still rings true:

> ... companies themselves are largely to blame. Long before the current medical attacks, the companies were building up suspicion in the consumer by the discredited 'health claims' in their ads... Such medicine-show claims may have given the smoker temporary confidence in one brand, but they also implied that cigarettes in general were distasteful, probably harmful, and certainly a 'problem'. When the scientists came along with their charges against cigarettes, the smoker was ready to accept them.

Later, the same organization said, 'There was every reason to believe that [most people over 18] would continue to smoke unless the tobacco promoters scared them out of their wits.'[82]

And that is how information works in competitive advertising.

Of course, 'less-bad' ads are not unique to cigarettes. They can probably be found wherever competitive advertising is allowed. I already described the health-claims-for-foods saga, which featured fat and cholesterol and the dangers of cancer and heart disease. Price advertising is another example. Prices are the most stubbornly negative product feature of all, because they represent the simple fact that the buyer must give up something else. There is no riper target for comparative advertising. When sellers advertise lower prices, competitors reduce their prices and advertise *that*, and soon a price war is in the works. This process so strongly favors

---

81 See *Wall Street Journal*, 13 January 1993, p B5, 'Bold Tobacco Ad on Ingredients Planned', by Laura Bird; *Wall Street Journal*, 10 October 1994, p A3, 'Reynolds Launches Menthol Cigarettes That Smell Better', by Fara Warner; and on the Eclipse, *Washington Post*, 27 May 1996, p A03, 'New Cigarette Clears the Smoke, but the Heat Is Still On', by John Schwartz.

82 *Consumer Reports*, February 1955, pp 63–64, and *The Consumers Union Report on Smoking and the Public Interest*, *op cit*, p 149.

consumers over the industry that one of the first things competitors do when they form a trade group is to propose an agreement to restrict or ban price advertising (if not ban *all* advertising). [83] When that fails, they try to get advertising regulators to stop price ads, an attempt that unfortunately often succeeds. This fascinating bit of regulation gone awry is the subject of a case study in chapter 7.

Someone is always trying to scare customers into switching brands out of fear for the product itself. The usual effect is to impress upon consumers what they do not like about the product. In 1991, when Americans were worried about insurance companies going broke, a few insurance firms advertised that they were more solvent than their competitors. This created quite a fuss in the industry. A *New York Times* article said, 'Amid the popularity of these campaigns, one concern is voiced by advertisers and their agencies: The ads might stir the very anxieties they are meant to calm.' The article quoted the well-known marketing consultant and author Al Ries: 'We call it "the implication of the opposite," ... "The rash of such advertising sends a message quite the opposite from the intended one – that all financial institutions are unsafe."' [84]

In May 1997, United Airlines began a new ad campaign that started out by reminding fliers of all the inconveniences that seem to crop up during air travel. As a *Wall Street Journal* story put it, 'Breaking with airline-industry clichés such as soaring planes and comfy seats, United Airlines' new ad campaign apologizes to road warriors for the pitiful state of air travel, and promises to make amends.' [85]

Health information is a fixture in 'less-bad' advertising. Ads for sleeping aids sometimes focus on the issue of whether they are habit-forming. [86] In March 1996, a medical journal reported that the pain reliever acetaminophen, the active ingredient in Tylenol, can cause liver damage in

---

83 As Adam Smith noted in his inimitable prose: 'People of the same trade seldom meet together, even for merriment and diversion, but the conversation ends in a conspiracy against the public, or in some contrivance to raise prices.' From the *Wealth of Nations*, as quoted in Heilbroner (1986), *op cit*, p 322.

84 *New York Times*, 3 September 1991, p D7, 'The Pitch: Safe Secure and Solvent', by Stuart Elliott.

85 *Wall Street Journal*, 16 May 1997, 'United's Ads Deploy Candor To Fly the Unfriendly Skies', by Susan Carey.

86 As in a 6 January 1996 television ad for Unison, with striking visuals on the advantages of a non-habit-forming sleeping potion.

heavy drinkers. This fact immediately became the focus of ads for Advil, a competing product. A public debate ensued, conducted through advertising, talk shows, news reports and pronouncements from medical authorities. The result was that consumers learned a lot more than they had known before about the fact *all* drugs have side effects. The press noted that this dispute may have helped consumers, but it hurt the pain reliever industry. [87]

Similar advertising campaigns, with similar results, continue to occur. In February 1997, the FDA recommended that the popular anti-allergy drug Seldane be removed from the market because it had a rare and avoidable side effect. A competitor whose drug, Claritin, did not have this side effect, immediately pounced. Full page ads began with huge headlines, 'Seldane May No Longer Be An Option; Claritin Is A Clear Choice.' The ad proceeded to describe the FDA's position. Again, consumers gained an enhanced respect for the possibility of side effects from popular drugs.[88]

More recently, Correctol, the number six laxative brand in the US (and sold by the manufacturer of Claritin), pointed out that yet another FDA advisory panel had concluded that an ingredient in Ex-Lax, the third best selling brand, might cause cancer, leading to the possibility that the FDA might remove the product from the market.[89] These ads prompted news stories about the competitive battle, about the products themselves, and most useful of all, about the flaws in the methods used to test for cancer-causing activity.[90]

And then there is political advertising. Some people think the American practice of televised mudslinging gives voters the impression that politicians are deceitful, self-seeking, and just possibly, concerned with something other than the public's welfare. The citizenry of other

---

87 Sources on this intriguing episode include *Business Week*, 25 March 1996, p 46, 'Calm Down and Take Two Aspirin', by Joseph Weber; and *New York Times*, 27 March 1996, p C11, 'How Safe are Tylenol and Advil? Helping Patients Sort Out the Risks', by Philip Hilts.

88 This ad appeared in the 27 January 1997 *Wall Street Journal* and other major newspapers. Also see *New York Times*, 12 June 1997, 'Schering-Plough's Rivals Accuse It of Unfair Ads', by Dana Canedy.

89 On laxatives, see *New York Times*, 12 June 1997, *op cit.*

90 *Business Week*, 30 June 1997, p 93, 'The Experiment That Could Clobber Ex-Lax', by Naomi Freundlich with Joseph Weber.

nations seem to be forming similar views as the American style of political campaigning spreads around the world.[91] Yet political candidates keep doing more advertising (unless restrained by law, as is common). The logic is simple. Each candidate believes advertising is necessary and each one does it in the hope of increasing his or her own vote. But the temptation to gain vote share through less-bad advertising ('I am not subservient to special interests, although my opponent certainly is') is just as strong as it is in ordinary markets. And there seems to be no shortage of issues on which to declare oneself to be less bad than one's opponent.

It should not be surprising, therefore, to find that evidence suggests that political advertising fails to increase voting and may even decrease it. A recent book on political advertising carried a title that summarizes the entire phenomenon, *Going Negative: How Political Advertisements Shrink and Polarize the Electorate.*[92] Political advertising appears to be another example of how competitive advertising can inform consumers about what is wrong with a product as well as what is right with it.

We have, then, a general rule: sellers will use comparative advertising when permitted to do so, even if it means spreading bad information about a product instead of favorable information. The mechanism usually takes the form of less-bad claims. One can hardly imagine a strategy more likely to give consumers the upper hand in the give and take of the marketplace. Less-bad claims are a primary means by which advertising serves markets and consumers rather than sellers. They completely refute the naive idea that competitive advertising will emphasize only the sellers' virtues while obscuring their problems.

Much of what has been set forth in this book assumes that consumers are alert for their own interests and eager to use advertising for their own purposes. What happens if advertising is directed at children or teenagers? It will be seen that advertising still works to the advantage of consumers, but does so in somewhat surprising ways.

---

91 See Lynda Lee Kaid and Christina Holtz-Bacha, eds, (1995) *Political Advertising in Western Democracies: Parties and Candidates on Television,* Sage Publications, especially p 146 on competitive dynamics, self-interest and the public good. The authors conclude, however, that negative political advertising is harmful rather than beneficial, because it undermines principles of broad public value.

92 By Stephen Ansolabehere and Shato Iyengar (1995), Free Press.

4 Advertising and Children

'All children were aware that the intent of each commercial was to sell beer... There was considerable skepticism about the promises that beer commercials make about the popularity, fun and good times to be had if you buy their brand of beer.' [93]

'The smart, active child viewer is the image behind much of the advertising industry's own research.' [94]

Most disputes about advertising come and go. But advertising to children always seems to be under fire. These attacks have arisen largely because of popular misunderstanding about the role of advertising in the life of children and adolescents.

The first and most essential point is that children and advertising do not comprise a single topic. Four-year-olds have little in common with ten-year-olds, who are also a lot different from sixteen-year-old adolescents. Lumping these age groups together makes no sense when analyzing the effects of advertising. One must at least deal separately with very young children.

What Do Children Know and When Do They Know It?

Serious research on how children view and use advertising seems to have begun during the intense debates over television advertising in the 1970s. A continuing stream of research has demonstrated that children learn at an early age what advertising is all about. A pioneering 1972 study found that second graders understand that advertising is designed to sell products, and

---

93 From a description of focus group interviews with fifth- and sixth-grade children, in Lawrence Wallack, Diana Cassady and Joel Grube (1990) 'TV Beer Commercials and Children: Exposure, Attention, Beliefs and Expectations About Drinking as an Adult', AAA Foundation for Traffic Safety.

94 Ellen Seiter (1993) *Sold Separately: Parents and Children in Consumer Culture*, New Brunswick, NJ: Rutgers University Press, p 107.

that slightly older children are already deeply skeptical of advertising claims. Asked whether 'commercials always tell the truth,' 66% of 8- to 10-year-olds said 'no' and 17%, 'sometimes.' For 11- and 12-year-olds, the tallies were 70% 'no' and 20% 'sometimes' (only 5% answered 'yes'). [95] Again, we encounter the skeptical 70% majority (see chapter 2); it is apparently in place by the age of 12.

Research published in 1974 examined first, third and fifth graders. By the fifth grade, awareness of the 'persuasive intent' of advertising had reached 99%, and 'perception of discrepancies between message and product.' 79%. The authors concluded that children had already constructed what consumer researchers refer to as 'cognitive defenses' against the persuasive power and intent of advertising. Later research has largely confirmed these early results.[96]

We can see that by the age 10 or so, children develop a full understanding of the purpose of advertising and equally important, an active suspicion of what advertisers say. Continuing research has buttressed and refined these results. Research published in 1978 found that adolescents grant little credibility to advertising. The researchers were surprised by an additional finding, that the level of skepticism was unrelated to the amount of television viewing. A 1982 study of 12- and 13-year-olds found deep skepticism of advertising in general and of specific advertising claims in particular. They concluded that '… almost two-thirds (62%) expect that advertisers often or always lie or cheat.' [97] A recent review of the research literature, in a volume published by the US federal government's National Institute for Alcoholism and Alcohol Abuse (NIAAA), concluded that '… the general dislike and skepticism for advertising may result in

---

95 Scott Ward (1972) 'Children's Reactions to Commercials', 12/2 *Journal of Advertising Research*, pp 37–45.

96 Thomas S Robertson and J R Rossiter (1974) 'Children and Commercial Persuasion: An Attribution Theory Analysis', 1/1 *Journal of Consumer Research*, pp 13–20. Also see the literature review in David W Stewart and Ronald Rice (1995) 'Non-traditional Advertising and Promotions in the Marketing of Alcoholic Beverages', in Susan E Martin, ed. *Research Monograph No 28: the Effects of the Mass Media on the Use and Abuse of Alcohol*, Washington, DC: NIAAA, pp 209–238

97 See Roy L Moore and George . Moschis (1978) 'Teenagers' Reactions to Advertising', 7 *Journal of Advertising*, pp 24–30; and C Linn, Tina de Benedictis, and Kevin Delucchi (1982) 'Adolescent Reasoning about Advertisements: Preliminary Investigations', 53 *Child Development*, pp 1599–1613.

adolescents tuning out most advertising they are exposed to, and may result in increased vigilance of advertising claims. This could result in adolescents being less influenced by advertising than adults.'[98]

Very Young Children

Probably the most persistent controversies concern children who are too young to shop. Children of ages four to seven, say, do not read newspapers and magazines. They were largely beyond the reach of advertising – until television arrived. TV advertising provided a new arrangement. Sellers could communicate directly to the child/consumer, who in turn could communicate with the parent/shopper. This development aroused fears that children, acting under the influence of a force they do not understand, would distort the family purchases against the family's own interests, while creating all sorts of tensions in the process. As will be seen shortly, some feared the worst. Advertising to children came to be seen as profoundly different from advertising in general, bereft of advertising's usual benefits and carrying more than the usual costs. The implication was that children and their families should be protected from receiving any advertising directed to children at all.

In the late 1970s, the FTC staff proposed a ban on all television advertising to children under the age of 8, and a ban on television advertising for sugared products targeted at children aged 8 through 12. This proposal never came close to enactment. The *Washington Post* editorial page, normally a friend of FTC regulation, declared that the agency was trying to become the 'national nanny.' Criticism of FTC over-reaching became widespread. Fighting to preserve its very existence, the FTC soon dropped its children's advertising scheme.[99]

Nonetheless, a few nations have done what the FTC only thought about doing. Greece prohibits toy advertising on television before 10pm. Sweden bans all toy advertising to children under the age of 12 and has

---

98 Stewart and Rice (1995), *op cit*, p 228.

99 This episode is recounted in Susan Foote and Robert Mnookin (1980) 'The "Kid Vid" Crusade', 61 *The Public Interest* (Fall), pp 90–105. Michael Pertschuk, the Chairman of the FTC during the late 1970s, provided his own colorful account in *Revolt Against Regulation: The Rise and Pause of the Consumer Movement* (University of California Press, 1982).

proposed that the European Commission extend the ban to the entire EU. Norway also forbids television advertising to children and has therefore essentially banned programming for children on its commercial stations; its attempt to apply its prohibition to cross-border broadcasting failed, however.[100] These measures reflect the long-held view that however useful advertising may be for adults, it has no value when children are involved.[101]

This dark view of advertising and young children is largely without foundation. To be sure, one can understand why parents would exaggerate the influence of advertising. They can monitor what their children see on television, but much of the child's social interactions occurs out of the parent's sight. With advertising so prominent, fear of its power can grow beyond reasonable bounds.[102] But experience has shown that advertising to children, like all advertising, works mainly to quicken the competitive process and to enhance the tendency for sellers to provide what buyers want. Of course, the marketing process with young children cannot be exactly the same as it is for selling to adolescents and adults. Information goes through different routes, and the family unit is of special importance. Nonetheless, the market's search for ways to supply what consumers want at lower prices is always at work with benefits to children and parents alike.

Toy advertising is a perfect example. When television advertising arrived in the United States in the 1950s – and this is a well-documented story – it transformed the toy market. Young consumers became more brand-conscious. They eagerly shared their insights with their parents, who soon knew exactly what to look for when they entered a toy store. Having focussed on specific items, parents fell into the habit of comparing prices. Retailers fell over themselves to cater to the new price-awareness. The result was one of the most striking episodes in the history of

---

100 Most of these details are taken from a 26 September 1996 briefing paper by the Advertising Association in London. On television programming in Norway, Jeffrey Goldstein quotes the 15 July 1993 *International Herald Tribune* as saying 'as a result TV2 has no specifically children's programming.' See his *Children and Advertising in Scandinavia*, prepared in 1995 for the Toy Manufacturers of Europe, Brussels, p 18.

101 See the debate in the March 1996 issue of *Commercial Communications*, published by DG XV of the EC.

102 See Jeffrey Goldstein (1994) Children and Advertising: Policy Implications of Scholarly Research, London: Advertising Association, p 17.

advertising. The march of television advertising from one metropolitan area to the next was followed by dropping toy prices.[103]

To anyone suspicious about how advertising affects competition, this must be an amazing story. Sellers advertised their brands directly to children. The children asked their parents to buy the toys they saw on TV without caring how much they cost. The parents went to the store looking for the brands their children wanted. Then what happened? A lot of people might assume that the parents encountered higher prices because demand had been increased through advertising targeted at an ignorant audience (children). But this is another case where popular expectations are mistaken. One must take into account the competitive process. The ads ratcheted up competition at the retail level, so much so that parents in search of heavily advertised toys actually found lower prices. It was a remarkable example of the indirect benefits of advertising, and it should be much better known than it is today.

The toy advertising story is part of a general pattern in advertising and prices, which is described at length in a case study in chapter 7.[104] Ad bans – and that is the topic here – protect manufacturers (especially domestic manufacturers) from competition, and particularly from new entrants. Less competition always means higher prices and less product variety.

No wonder foreign toy manufacturers point out that children in Sweden and Greece have far fewer toys to choose from than children in European nations with toy advertising. The Greek law, in fact, is apparently protectionist by design. A close observer from the international toy manufacturing industry has described several tortuous years in which the Greek ban was rescinded (in the face of objections based on EU law), reinstated, rescinded again, and finally placed on the books again in 1994.

---

103 The seminal source on toy advertising and television was written by a toy manufacturing executive who became a scholar of the history of advertising and then served on the staff of the Bureau of Economics at the FTC. See Robert Steiner (1973) 'Does Advertising Lower Consumer Prices?' 37 *Journal of Marketing*, pp 19–26.

104 Steiner's pioneering work on advertising and prices has been extended by Albion and by Reekie. See Mark Albion (1983) *Advertising's Hidden Effects: Manufacturers' Advertising And Retail Pricing*, Auburn House; and W Duncan Reekie (1982) 'Advertising and Price', 1/2 *International Journal of Advertising*, pp 131–141; reprinted in W Duncan Reekie (1988) *Issues in Advertising*, Cape Town, South Africa: Juta.

The observer remarked, 'it was known that the association of indigenous Greek toy distributors and importers had lobbied for the ban as a trade protection measure as they had done on the previous occasions. Public statements were made to the effect that Greek distributors needed protection from international toy businesses penetrating the Greek market and close collaboration was apparent between representatives of the association and the then Greek Trade Minister.' He added that in the next year or so, international firms lost about 40% of the advertised brand business in Greece.[105]

Here, in general terms, is how advertising seems to work for young children and their parents. Advertising interacts with the numerous other factors that shape the child's maturing preferences and the child's ability to articulate these preferences. The information and persuasion from advertising also contribute to the child's growing knowledge and appreciation of what the world can offer. Advertising therefore blends with other far more numerous and forceful influences on the growing child. Some of these other influences are bound to conflict with parental desires, controls and financial constraints. This makes it easy to blame advertising for the inevitable tensions of raising children in an imperfect world. But these are problems that parents can and must deal with directly, whether there is advertising or no advertising. The problems are largely internal to the family and are subject to direct parental influence. There is little reason to think that an end to advertising would substantially ease the tasks of raising a child.

Now look beyond the family unit. Advertising provides its greatest benefits precisely where children and their parents can do the least for themselves: forcing the market to provide better products more cheaply. However powerful and beneficial is the influence of individual parents over their child, those same parents have but a trivial impact on the market at large. To get improvements in the marketplace, competition among sellers is necessary. Advertising bolsters competition, bringing better products at

---

105 From a paper by Peter Waterman of the Toy Manufacturers of Europe in Advertising Association (1997) *Barriers to British Export Competitiveness in Europe: The Commercial Communications Sector*, papers from a seminar held 20 September 1996, pp 41–45.

lower prices – even for toys used by youngsters who have yet to learn the basic elements of markets, advertising and competition.

All this is borne out in the research. In the home and in the life of the child, advertising is a slight force in comparison to the parents, siblings, teachers and friends the child sees every day. In the marketplace, however, advertising can make the difference between better, cheaper toys (including educational toys, of course) and fewer, more expensive toys. The irony is notable. Advertising to children, so often believed to be an exception to rule that advertising makes markets work better, actually provides one of the more compelling examples of the benefits of advertising.

Adolescents and Advertising

What about adolescents, who are old enough to do most of their own buying? Adolescents are exposed to a lot of advertising (mainly on TV, but also in print, on billboards and especially, on the radio). They can use advertising just like adults do. A natural question is whether adolescents are capable of handling advertising as opposed to being victimized by it.

The evidence reveals that adolescents are media-savvy consumers. By the time they reach their teen years, children have partaken of the views and insights of the larger adult consumer society. These include an appreciation of advertising's purpose, and a life-long skepticism toward its claims. These tools are well established *before* youngsters become independently active consumers.[106] This process is completely natural. Indeed, it could hardly be otherwise. An essential part of the complex process of growing from child to adult is the gradual comprehension of products, markets and prices. An understanding of advertising forms part of this larger understanding of the economic environment.

But these adolescent consumers do not yet have the freedom of adults. Their funds are far more limited (with parents doing most of the major purchasing and most of the saving for college and other future expenses), transportation is more restricted, they are still living at home and (for the most part, at least) they are still subject to powerful parental influence and

---

[106] See the citations in the first section of this chapter, and the section in chapter 2 on consumer skepticism.

controls. The main lessons about advertising are therefore absorbed at a time when the costs of error and misunderstanding are still relatively modest.

All this leaves little room for the idea that advertising shapes headstrong teens into docile consumers. Nonetheless, controversy remains.

The greatest public tension is over advertising for products that are illegal for children or which society disapproves for teens (and usually, for adults as well). These include tobacco and alcohol. How strong an influence is advertising? If it had the force of family and friends, advertising could be a significant cause of smoking and drinking. But advertising has nothing like that kind of power. When it comes to fundamental decisions in life – and whether to smoke or drink is for most people a very fundamental decision – advertising is a weak force indeed in the life of the teenager.

This is evident from several streams of research. For decades, research on the causes of smoking and drinking proceeded with no attention whatever to the influence of advertising. This was not because scholars had no interest in advertising, but rather because the social psychology discipline suggested there was little reason to think advertising would be important, and there were strong reasons to believe other factors were at work. Early on, overwhelming evidence indicated that youthful decisions about smoking and drinking are dominated by such forces as parents (parental smoking is an excellent predictor of youth smoking) and especially, peers (an even stronger predictor).

It was not until advertising became controversial that scholars began a serious attempt to implicate advertising in the initiation of drinking or smoking. When the US banned broadcast advertising for cigarettes in 1970, a psychologist who was affiliated with the American Cancer Society (and was a vigorous opponent of smoking) pointed out that there were no data whatsoever to support the notion that advertising was a cause of smoking. He then conducted his own research on youth smoking and could find no connection with advertising.[107]

---

107 See Eugene E Levitt (1970) 'The Television Cigarette Commercial: Teenage Transducer or Paper Tiger?', 45 *Yale Scientific Magazine*, (October) pp 10–15; and Eugene E Levitt (1977) 'The TV Cigarette Ad Ban: Unexpected Fallout', 2 *World Smoking and Health*, (Fall) pp 4–8.

The same pattern applies to research on drinking. In a comprehensive review of the literature published in 1978 on the causes of drinking and alcoholism, the authors stated in the section on teenage drinking that 'It is important to note at the outset that not one of the studies reviewed considered advertising as a relevant variable in teenage drinking.'[108]

Research continues to show that youthful decisions on whether or not to drink or smoke tend to be shaped by basic social forces, not advertising. This is evident from numerous literature reviews, including the various US Surgeon General's reports on smoking and health. For example, the 1979 report said after reviewing the research literature on youth smoking, 'predictably, the influences most frequently cited include the role of the family, pressures from peer groups, formal education programs, and the effects of messages transmitted through the mass media [not advertising].' A 1981 literature review by members of Norway's National Council of Smoking and Health noted, 'Most of the scientific literature in this field consistently agrees that social factors by far represent the dominating influence as regards starting to smoke,' and the authors cited the 1977 report of the Royal College of Physicians. More recently, a survey article by a Dutch economist concluded, 'The literature makes clear that peer influence, especially from peers of the same sex, is the pre-eminent factor in the onset of smoking experimentation and the maintenance of smoking.'[109]

Over and over again, the literature on youth and alcohol reaches the same result. A renowned scholar at Canada's government-funded Addiction Research Foundation concluded in 1988 that '[b]ecause factors such as price and social influences most affect decisions to drink, the influence of advertising is likely to be relatively small.' In fact, his review of the literature found no significant influence at all from advertising. A more recent survey

---

108 David Pittman and M Dow Lambert (1978) *Alcohol, Alcoholism, and Advertising: A Preliminary Investigation of Asserted Associations*, Washington University, p 43.

109 See US Department of Health, Education and Welfare, Public Health Service (1979) *Smoking and Health: Report of the Advisory Committee to the Surgeon General of the Public Health Service*, Pub No (PHS) 79–50066, US GPO, Washington, DC. The Norwegian study is L Aaro, A Hauknes, and L Berglund (1981) Smoking Among Norwegian Schoolchildren, 1975–1980, 22 *Scandinavian Journal of Psychology*, pp 297–309. The last quotation is from W Fred van Raaij (1990) The Effect of Marketing Communication on the Initiation of Juvenile Smoking, 9 *International Journal of Advertising*, pp 15–36.

concluded that '… there is general consensus that parents and peers are far more powerful influences on consumption behavior for a wide variety of products [including alcoholic beverages] than is advertising [citations omitted].' In 1995, a comprehensive review of the literature on drinking by inner-city youth described a similar set of influences, with advertising barely even mentioned. A new federal government 'research-based' guide to preventing drug use by children (including underage drinking) is essentially devoid of references to the influence of advertising.[110] Even the work of scholars dedicated to isolating the effects of alcohol advertising has emphasized the far more fundamental role of peers and other cultural influences.[111]

Nonetheless, the past two decades have seen numerous attempts (many of them government-funded) to assess the connections, if any, between advertising and the consumption of tobacco and alcohol. These efforts have not contributed much to our understanding of why young people drink or smoke, but at least they have added some knowledge about how advertising works.

One finding is that teens greet tobacco and alcohol advertising with pretty much the same skepticism of sellers' motives that they and their parents bring to advertising generally. The authors of a 1981 study of Australian children, for example, concluded that their research 'leaves little doubt as to the opinion of this group of Australian 10- and 11-year-olds: Cigarette advertisements are intended to lead people to take up smoking …' Roughly similar attitudes have been found repeatedly in later studies.[112]

110 The Addiction Research Foundation report was Reginald Smart (1988) 'Does Alcohol Advertising Affect Overall Consumption? A Review of Empirical Studies', 49/4 *Journal of Studies on Alcohol*, pp 314–323. The 'general consensus' quote is from a wide-ranging review by David Stewart and Ronald Rice (1994) 'Adolescent's Response to Tobacco and Beer Advertising: In Search of the Causal Linkage Between Advertising Exposure and Product Attitudes and Usage', presented at the Public Policy and Marketing Conference, Washington, DC, May 1993. On inner city youth, see Jennifer Epstein, Gilbert Botvin, Tracy Diaz, and Steven Schinke (1995) 'The Role of Social Factors and Individual Characteristics in Promoting Alcohol Use among Inner-City Minority Youths', 56 *Journal of Studies on Alcohol*, pp 39–46. Also see US Department of Health and Human Services, National Institute on Drug Abuse (1997) *Preventing Drug Use Among Children and Adolescents: A Research-Based Guide*.

111 See G B Hastings, A M Mackintosh, and P P Aitken (1992) 'Is Alcohol Advertising Reaching the People It Shouldn't Reach?', 51/1 *Health Education Journal*, pp 38–42.

112 See Debra Ringold (1995) 'Social Criticisms of Target Marketing: Process or Product?', 38/4 *American Behavioral Scientist* (February), pp 578–592.

Research by analysts who are hostile to alcoholic beverage advertising has found the same thing, as illustrated by the quotation on beer ads at the start of this chapter.

Findings like this rule out the most obvious possibility, that advertising simply seduces young people into mistakes through sheer charm combined with subtle obfuscation of the facts. We know that if advertising is to have even a chance at exerting a profound effect on the most important decisions faced by youth, it is going to have to work very hard, and even then it will face little hope of success. Before concluding that advertising actually achieves such a challenging task, one should examine the empirical connections between advertising and consumption.

A large body of research has investigated the influence of advertising on the consumption of tobacco and alcohol. Much of this research asks whether there is a relationship between attitudes toward advertising for a particular product and the use of that product. This approach is bound to be inconclusive. It would be surprising if such a relationship did *not* exist. It is well known that people tend to pay more attention to ads for products they use: 'Volvo owners watch Volvo ads,' as the saying goes.[113] Research does in fact find that teenagers who drink or are interested in drinking enjoy alcohol ads more than other teens. The relationship is usually not a strong one, however, and is sometimes slight or nonexistent. More to the point, these results provide no reason to think that the ads *caused* drinking. It is more likely that things work in the opposite direction: people who drink or want to drink pay more attention to alcohol ads (or there could be a third factor that leads to both drinking and attention to advertising).[114]

The possibility of reverse causation in surveys on attitudes and consumption is now so well recognized that serious researchers routinely warn readers that, as one widely cited article put it, 'the possibility that drinkers may pay more attention to messages about alcohol beverages than

---

113 Gerald J S Wilde (1993) 'Effects of Mass Media Communications on Health and Safety Habits: An Overview of Issues and Evidence', 88 *Addiction*, pp 983–996.

114 See John E Calfee and Carl Scheraga (1994) 'The Influence of Advertising on Alcohol Consumption: Review of the Evidence and An Econometric Analysis of Four European Nations', *International Journal of Advertising*, vol.13, no 4, pp 287–310, and citations therein.

non-drinkers confounds any relations that such surveys might find between exposure and behavior.'[115]

Survey research therefore leaves no reason to think advertising is a factor in teenagers' decisions about alcohol and cigarettes, beyond the obvious fact that advertising shapes preferences among brands. But you, the reader, should now consider yourself to have been warned. Sometime in the near future you will probably hear about a survey in which it was discovered that people who pay more attention to alcohol ads also consume more alcohol – except the product may be tobacco instead of alcohol, or it may be diet soda or personal computers or Internet service providers or rock and roll groups or who knows what else. If you read the fine print in these survey reports, you will almost always find a scholarly disclaimer to the point that these results do not tell us why these consumers use more of the product. But the fine print probably will not make it into the news.

A special niche in alcohol advertising research is occupied by 'experiments.' These are studies in which subjects are randomly divided into two or three groups. One group views alcoholic beverage ads while the others view ads for other products. The goal is to see whether the groups who saw alcohol ads buy or drink more alcohol, or develop more positive attitudes toward drinking. Most experiments have used college students, although at least one used 5th and 8th graders. The consistent finding is a lack of effect from advertising. The authors of the most recent study concluded 'the failure of beer commercials to create positive alcohol expectancies is consistent with limited and null findings of previous investigations. Research to date does not support a ban on alcohol advertising.'[116]

---

115 L R Lieberman and M A Orlandi (1987) 'Alcohol Advertising and Adolescent Drinking', 12/1 *Alcohol Health Research World*, pp 30–33. Also see E M Adlaf and P M Kohn (1989) 'Alcohol Advertising, Consumption and Abuse: A Covariance-Structural Modelling Look at Strickland's Data', 84 *British Journal of Addiction*, pp 749–757, who say on p 749, 'Demonstrations of positive correlations between advertising exposures and alcohol consumption in survey studies have ambiguous causal implications, even with statistical control of other variables [citations omitted].'

116 See Lipsitz, Brake, Vincent, and Winters (1993) 'Another Round for the Brewers: Television Ads and Children's Alcohol Expectancies', 23/6 *Journal of Applied Social Psychology*, p 439. Earlier research is summarized in that article and in Calfee and Scheraga (1994), *op cit*.

A final line of research is the most relevant of all. It does not look specifically at teenagers, but examines the relationship between total advertising and total consumption. If advertising has no effect on total consumption of alcohol and tobacco, there is little reason to think it induces teenagers to start drinking or smoking. After all, if advertising did have such an effect, it would show up pretty quickly in consumption data as youngsters move into their twenties, when consumption is often at the highest levels.

The research on advertising and product consumption is reviewed in the next chapter. To preview the results, the bottom line is simple: There is no discernible connection between advertising and consumption of either tobacco or alcohol. This large body of research essentially rules out the possibility of a significant influence from advertising on youthful decisions about whether to smoke or drink.

It should now be clear that advertising to children and adolescents should not be nearly as controversial as it is. Advertising works to the advantage of children and families, sometimes strikingly so. On the other hand, the social problems of youth that command the attention of parents and governments are well beyond the reach of both the creators of advertising and the regulators of advertising.

5 What Do Advertising Bans Accomplish?

'The anti-smoking forces were victims of the credulous belief that the tobacco industry would not have spent one quarter of a billion dollars a year on air media advertising unless that effort paid off by opening fresh markets. This is a common misconception.'[117]

'Norwegians Continue to Smoke 20 Years After Tobacco Ad Ban'[118]

'In the ornate Negotiation Room at the headquarters of the China National Tobacco Corp. in Beijing, two renowned anti-smoking crusaders and executives of the world's largest producer of cigarettes forged an unlikely alliance ...'[119]

Why Ad Bans?

Bans on advertising for specific products or services have always been common. They used to be a standard feature in so-called codes of ethics for physicians, attorneys, accountants and other professionals. In the United States, at least, such protectionist ad bans have largely disappeared under pressure from the FTC.[120] The impulse to use ad bans to stifle competition is always with us, however. Examples include the toy advertising ban in Greece, bans on price ads and most comparative claims in Germany and other nations, and persistent attempts by various US states to restore restrictions on attorney advertising.

---

117 Eugene Levitt of the American Cancer Society, on why the US Congress banned cigarette advertising on television in 1970 in a fruitless attempt to reduce smoking. See Levitt (1977) *op cit.*

118 Headline in the *Wall Street Journal*, 10 June 1997.

119 *Washington Post*, 20 November 1996, p A1, 'Big Tobacco's Global Reach: Vast China Market Key to Smoking Disputes', by Glenn Frankel and Steven Mufson.

120 See the citations in the discussion in chapter 1 on the FTC's policy of attacking restrictions on advertising by private groups. The previously cited 1984 FTC report by Jacobs, *et al*, contains useful material on the history of professional restrictions on attorney advertising.

There is another, more modern source of ad bans. Here, the idea is to ban advertising in the hopes of solving social problems such as smoking and alcohol abuse. The premise is that advertising for cigarettes, alcohol and perhaps other products is inherently misleading or unfair because it leads to the use or abuse of these products.

The attempt to solve social problems by banning advertising is the topic of this chapter. We might as well start with tobacco.

The Most Popular Ad Ban: Tobacco

In 1975, Norway banned cigarette advertising in order to reduce smoking, especially by young people. Consumption immediately declined, but a study by Norway's National Council of Smoking and Health scotched the idea that the ban was the reason. Prices and social influences were also at work, the Council noted, and the decline in consumption was probably caused by the massive publicity surrounding the ban, along with a very large tax increase on cigarettes that accompanied it. Since then, progress against smoking in Norway has been disappointing. A substantial decline in the percentage of men who smoke has been partly offset by an increase in consumption of cigarettes per male smoker. Moreover, the percentage of women smoking has not budged, and again, those who do smoke are smoking more per day. A modest decline in total consumption is easily explained by dramatic tax increases that have driven the price to about seven US dollars per pack, about three and one-half times what US smokers pay – hence the *Wall Street Journal* headline quoted above.[121]

Norway was a pioneer, but it is no longer alone. What Norway failed to achieve with its ad ban, other nations have failed to achieve with their own ad bans. Finland imposed a partial ban on cigarette advertising in 1978. Smoking by teenagers and women has remained essentially unchanged in the 19 years since, while smoking rates by adult males declined modestly from 35% to 27%. New Zealand passed an ad ban in 1990 amid clamorous debate and sincere assurances from anti-smoking proponents that the ban would discourage smoking. Nevertheless, the percentage of adult New Zealanders who smoke has remained stuck at 27%. In 1989, Canada passed

---

121 The Norwegian study was Aaro, Hauknes, and Berglund (1981), *op cit.*

a comprehensive ban after much impassioned lobbying and debate. The ban was ruled unconstitutional on free speech grounds by a judge who found that the government had not provided credible evidence that bans reduce consumption. Despite this ruling, the ban has remained in place during court appeals, legislative deliberations, and negotiations with the industry. But the judge had it right. There was no reason to expect the ban to reduce smoking, and it did not reduce smoking. When the ban took effect in 1990, 29% of Canadians smoked. In 1994, after four years of the ad ban plus mammoth tax increases, 30% smoked.[122]

And what about the United States, arguably home to the least regulated and most vigorous cigarette advertising in the Western world? Between 1976 (the first year after Norway implemented its ad ban) and 1990, US consumption (in grams of tobacco per adult ages 15 and over) decreased from 4,342 grams to 3,020. This 30% reduction was achieved without significant new restrictions on ads, and without dramatic increases in taxes. Meanwhile, in Norway, per capita consumption declined by 1%, from 1,937 grams to 1,918. Finnish consumption *increased* from 1,908 to 2,070.[123] Also notable is the fact that per capita smoking in the advertising-sparse post-communist nations of Poland and Hungary has long been much higher than it was in those bastions of slick advertising, namely the US, Australia and Canada.[124]

This suggests that ad bans do not reduce smoking. This is confirmed by a recent analysis of data for 22 developed nations during the years 1964–1990. If one compares per capita cigarette consumption in nations that imposed bans (beginning with Iceland in 1971, then Norway in 1975, Finland in 1978, Italy and Portugal in 1983, and Canada in 1988/1989), one finds that consumption dropped more rapidly in the non-ban countries

122 Details about Finland, New Zealand and Canada are from the useful newspaper article that provided the quotation at the start of this chapter: 'Norwegians Continue to Smoke 20 Years After Tobacco Ad Ban', *Wall Street Journal*, 10 June 1997. The Canadian judge's decision has been printed with commentaries in John C Luik, ed (1991) *Freedom of Expression: The Case Against Tobacco Advertising Bans: A Landmark Decision*, Ontario, Canada: Gray Matters Press.

123 These data are from Michael J Stewart (1993) 'The Effect on Tobacco Consumption of Advertising Bans in OECD Countries', *International Journal of Advertising*, v.12, p 155; reprinted in Luik and Waterson (1996), *op cit*, pp 275–302.

124 *New York Times*, 6 June 1994, p D1, 'R J Reynolds Woos Polish Smokers', by Jane Perlez.

than in any of the ban countries except for Canada, which also increased prices by 18%. A statistical analysis, taking into account standard economic variables such as prices and income, revealed that ad bans were in fact weakly associated with *higher*, not lower consumption.[125]

Have cigarette ad bans therefore fallen out of fashion? Not at all, for two reasons. First, anti-smoking activists have not lost their faith in ad bans, which after all are much easier to bring off than changing the hearts and minds of parents and peers. Second, ad bans are good for business if you happen to be well established in the marketplace and fearful of competition from new entrants.

This thinking has made for some very strange bedfellows. In Asia, with its proliferation of newly liberated economies, nation after nation has passed or maintained cigarette ad bans with the support of anti-smoking advocates working in concert with entrenched cigarette manufacturers.[126]

The best example of this bizarre phenomenon is China. In 1994, two prominent tobacco opponents, one a long-time activist living in Hong Kong and the other a famous epidemiologist from Oxford University, sat down with the leader of what is by far the world's largest cigarette manufacturer. That manufacturer is the Chinese state-owned tobacco monopoly, with a stable of some 500(!) brands and an annual output more than three times the size of the entire annual consumption in the United States.

The activists told the head of the tobacco monopoly that what he needed was an ad ban to fend off western brands preparing to invade the newly opening Chinese market. The manufacturer heartily agreed, and the deal was done. I am afraid it was a bad deal, however, for the anti-tobacco

---

125 Again, the analysis is from Stewart (1993), *op cit.*

126 One example is Thailand. 'Led by Prakit and fellow physician Hatai Chitanondh, a senior official in the Thai Public Health Ministry, the counterattack [against the effort of American firms to gain market share through advertising] was aided by anti-smoking activists from other parts of Asia and from the United States. Invoking Thai nationalist sentiment and economic self-interest, *they enlisted the support of the government and the state-run tobacco monopoly.*' [emphasis added], *Washington Post*, 'Big Tobacco's Global Reach: Thailand Resists US Brand Assault', by Glenn Frankel, 18 November 1996, p A01. The article provides considerable detail on this episode, and refers to similar political battles in other Asian countries.

activists. The manufacturer got what he wanted, which was protection from competition and from irritating demands by smokers for the modern low-yield filter cigarettes that smokers everywhere want. The anti-smoking activists, of course, wanted a new constraint on cigarette consumption, but what they got instead was just another ad ban.[127]

One goal of anti-smoking groups will surely be met, however. The ad ban will retard Chinese smokers from switching to western brands. The Chinese will therefore ingest far more tar and nicotine than they otherwise would. A consistent feature of American and other western brands – whether the product is tobacco, alcohol, or exercise equipment and even many foods – is a focus on lightness, moderation and health. For drinks, this means less alcohol (from spirits to wine, from wine to beer) or even moving from alcoholic drinks to fruit juice and bottled water. For cigarettes, western advertising and marketing brings effective filters, competition to reduce tar and nicotine yield, and the subtle but insistent emphasis on health that necessarily emerges from 'less-bad' competition. A 1994 *New York Times* headline summarized things neatly: 'R J Reynolds Woos Polish Smokers: exploiting a trend *away* from popular pungent cigarettes' [emphasis added].[128] Ad bans sacrifice all this in the vain hope that the ban will reduce consumption.

How can we be so sure that cigarette ad bans do not reduce consumption? Because the effects of cigarette advertising are among the most analyzed topics in the economics of advertising, and the results overwhelmingly find no substantial effect from advertising on consumption (and usually no discernible effect at all). This research does not necessarily involve examining the effects of actual bans on advertising (which historically have been rare in large nations). Rather, one analyzes data through time, taking into account advertising, consumption, cigarette prices, personal income and other relevant variables. Then one can see what happens after large changes in the volume of advertising.

127 This episode is recounted in *The Washington Post*, 20 November 1996, *op cit.*
128 The headline is from the 6 June 1994 *New York Times, op cit.* On international comparisons of types of cigarettes, see Jean Boddewyn (1986) *Tobacco Advertising Bans and Consumption in 16 Countries*, New York, International Advertising Association. Regarding alcohol, the section below on alcohol ad bans provides citations on the changing East German drinks market.

This type of research, the oldest and most rigorous approach to assessing the effects of advertising on consumption, demonstrates two points. First, study after study of nation after nation has failed to uncover a significant relationship between cigarette advertising and consumption. Second, if such a relationship existed, we should have found it by now. The gyrations in advertising volume have been so large, and the disparities among nations so great, that it is now quite unlikely that advertising actually has a substantial but heretofore undetected effect on per capita consumption.

For example, recent comprehensive econometric analyses of the US market and the UK market – the latter analysis performed by a branch of the Department of Health, which obtained detailed proprietary information from the industry in order to overcome shortcomings in previous work – have found that large changes in the volume of cigarette advertising have no significant effect on consumption. Analyses of other nations such as Australia, Spain, Greece and South Korea reach similar results.[129]

It is unfortunate that the intellectual environment surrounding tobacco and health has become so politically charged that government agencies can choose to ignore the best available research on the effects of advertising. When the FDA issued its proposed regulations for tobacco advertising and promotion, it had to provide a review of the evidence on the effects of advertising. The FDA's review simply ignored the numerous statistical analyses of the American and British cigarette markets. None of the work described here was mentioned in the FDA document. Instead, the FDA review concentrated on survey research, which touches upon the effects of advertising on brand shares but certainly does not address whether

---

129 The most recent and most rigorous study of the US market is George Franke (1994) 'US Cigarette Demand, 1961–1990: Econometric Issues, Evidence, and Implications', 30 *Journal of Business Research*, pp 33–41. The UK report, referred to as the 'Smee Report' after its lead author, is UK Department of Health, Economics and Operational Research Division, 'Effect of Tobacco Advertising on Tobacco Consumption: A Discussion Document Reviewing the Evidence', October 1992. Numerous statistical studies are reviewed in Martyn Duffy, 'Econometric Studies of Advertising, Advertising Restrictions and Cigarette Demand: A Survey,' in Luik and Waterson (1996), *op cit.* That volume also includes a useful analysis by Luik of the Smee Report (which included a survey of the literature as well as original research).

advertising causes consumption, plus one or two statistical studies that did not examine advertising data at all.[130]

In fact, there actually is a way to use advertising to reduce tobacco consumption. The solution is not to ban tobacco advertising, but to increase the freedom for anti-smoking products to advertise. The United States has recently moved nicotine patches and nicotine gum from prescription to over-the-counter status. The result has been a flood of advertising that focuses, not on the horrors of smoking (which surveys indicated are already completely ensconced in the minds of just about everyone) but on how to deal with all the difficulties of quitting.[131]

This is better than banning cigarette advertising. It is even better than government-subsidized anti-smoking ads. Those tend to emphasize the horrors of smoking and the immorality of tobacco companies. Moreover, public-supported advertisements tend to represent the efforts of advertising agencies to demonstrate their expertise in creating ads, rather than in getting people to quit smoking or not to start smoking.[132]

Advertising, Alcohol Consumption and Alcohol Abuse

Another worldwide target of ad bans is alcoholic beverages. Although the product is very different from cigarettes, the essential workings of advertising bans are similar. Many nations prohibit some or all alcohol advertising on broadcast media. In 1979, Sweden implemented a complete alcohol ad ban for all media. Twelve years later in 1991, as the French wine

---

130 The FDA document is 'Regulations Restricting the Sale and Distribution of Cigarettes and Smokeless Tobacco Products to Protect Children and Adolescents', 60/155 *Federal Register* 41314, Docket No 95N–0253, 11 August 1995. A critique of the FDA's review of the literature is available in 'Comments from the American Advertising Federation to the Food and Drug Administration,' Docket No 95N–0253, December 1995, available from the FDA or from the AAF at 1101 Vermont Ave, NW, Suite 500, Washington, DC 20005.

131 See *Advertising Age*, 11 August 1997. Smoking cessation drugs now include the anti-depressant Wellbutrin reformulated as a smoking cessation pill, in addition to nicotine in the form of patches and chewing gum.

132 This was recently pointed out by one of the most insightful practitioners of social marketing: '... the [advertising] agency may focus most of its energies on being creative – hoping to win a major award for its work – and in the process, lose sight of the program's basic strategy. Many agencies seem to take on [social marketing] campaigns in order to win creativity awards. This is not necessarily good for the program.' Alan Andreasen (1995) *Marketing Social Change: Changing Behavior to Promote Health, Social Development, and the Environment*, Josey-Bass Publishers, p 297.

industry stood quietly deep in thought (no doubt pondering the dramatic recent increases in both advertising and market share by imported drinks manufacturers), the French National Assembly passed the 'loi Evin,' named after the health minister who proposed it. The loi Evin severely restricted alcohol advertising, and it did so with the explicit purpose of reducing the health costs of alcohol abuse.[133]

Here is what has happened in France and Sweden in recent years. Figure 1 presents data on alcoholic beverage consumption in these two nations during the past 24 years. The graph indicates the dates when Sweden implemented its complete ad ban, and France, its loi Evin. I suspect that if these dates had been omitted, readers would have a difficult time guessing which nation instituted an ad ban in the late 1970s.

Several things are clear from the French and Swedish data. In France, consumption dropped rapidly from 1976 on, even though advertising was relatively untouched by regulation before 1991. In Sweden, consumption remained essentially unchanged despite 15 years of a comprehensive ad ban.

Neither the Swedish ad ban nor the French loi Evin has had a visible effect on consumption. In fact, per capita alcohol consumption in France peaked in the mid-1950s. The decline halted by the early 1970s, only to resume even more strongly in the late 1970s.

133 M Evin stated that he was submitting 'a project intended to prevent illness and suffering by many of our fellow citizens' ('un projet de nature à éviter la maladie et le malheur à beaucoup de nos concitoyens'). Later, M Evin even described the advertising restrictions as necessary for improving public health and reducing mortality ('tous ses membres [de la communauté scientifique] estiment que l'interdiction ... partielle de la publicité en faveur de l'alcool est nécessaire si l'on veut vraiment améliorer l'état sanitaire du pays et diminuer la mortalité.' See Assemblée Nationale, Compte Rendu Analytique Officiel, 1ère séance du lundi 25 juin 1990. *Marketing Week*, March 2, 1990, p 20, reported that 'French health minister Claude Evin wants to cut down on his country's national health service bill by banning ads for cigarettes and alcohol.'

FIGURE 1: ADVERTISING RESTRICTIONS AND ALCOHOL CONSUMPTION
IN FRANCE AND SWEDEN, 1971–1994

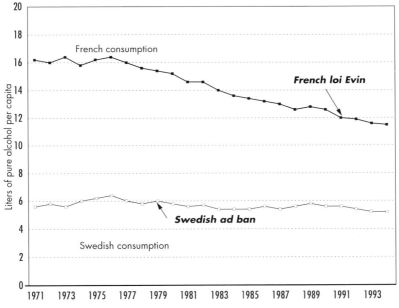

Data from *World Drink Trends*, 1995 ed.

At first, these reductions in French consumption were driven by the
increased availability of clean drinking water. Then changing lifestyles took
over. Adults began to drop the habit of drinking liqueurs after dinner.
Younger consumers gradually abandoned the traditional French preference
for wine with every meal and adopted the more international preference
for beer, soft drinks, and 'lighter' products generally.[134] The downward
slide in consumption continued through 1994 virtually as it had in the
fifteen years before the loi Evin was enacted, despite the fact that advertising
(which had tripled in the years leading up to 1991) declined precipitously
after the law was passed (see Figure 2 for advertising expenditures).

134 *Cf* Brewers Association of Canada (1993) *International Survey. Alcoholic Beverage Taxation and Control
Policies*, 8th ed, by R Brazeau and Nancy Burr, edited by Margo Dewar and H Collins, pp 129ff.
On the changing tastes and consumption of East Germans, see 15/91 IFO-Schnelldienst, pp 8–12,
'Die Ostdeutschen dürsten nach Westgetränken' ('East Germans Thirst after Western Drinks') (1991),
and ibid, 24/92, p 17–20, 'Ostdeutsche übernehmen suzehends westliche Trinkgewohnheiten',
(East Germans develop increasingly Western drinking habits'). The latter reports discuss the growth
in East German consumption of wine and champagne, coffee, fruit juice, and mineral water.

Now look at liver disease (including cirrhosis). Figure 2 presents French data on alcoholic beverage advertising and death rates from chronic liver disease and cirrhosis of the liver.

FIGURE 2: LIVER DISEASE AND ALCOHOL ADVERTISING, FRANCE, 1971–1992

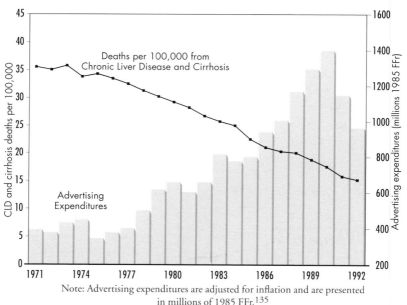

Note: Advertising expenditures are adjusted for inflation and are presented in millions of 1985 FFr.[135]

These data are compelling. Death rates from liver disease in France have declined very rapidly, and the decline started at about the same time that advertising expenditures began a long period of *increases*. Between 1975 and 1990, advertising expenditures (corrected for inflation by putting all amounts in terms of 1985 French francs) increased by approximately 250%, from about 400 million FFr to about 1,400 million FFr. At the same time, liver disease mortality declined by half, from 35 per 100,000 to 17.5. This remarkable improvement in public health continued at exactly the same rate, no better and no worse, when the loi Evin suddenly caused advertising expenditures to drop sharply to about 950 million FFr between 1990 and 1992.

135 Source for data: J E Calfee (1996) 'Some Notes on the Effects of Alcoholic Beverage Advertising in Europe', printed in English and French in the *Bulletin de l'office international de la vigne et du vin*, September–October.

The lack of correlation between advertising and liver disease could hardly be more striking. It provides a persuasive reason to believe that the loi Evin has had nothing whatever to do with preventing alcohol abuse. The new law only succeeded in reducing advertising expenditures. Indeed, one might conclude that the main and totally unexpected result of the loi Evin was to demonstrate the futility of ad bans as a tool for attacking social problems such as alcohol abuse.[136]

Is it possible that the French loi Evin really did reduce consumption, but its effects were disguised by other events, perhaps changes in prices or consumer income? I investigated this question in a statistical analysis of the French market.[137] Figure 3 presents data on alcohol consumption, alcohol advertising, alcoholic beverage prices, and disposable income in France during the years 1971–1994.

Figure 3: French Alcohol Market, 1971–1994

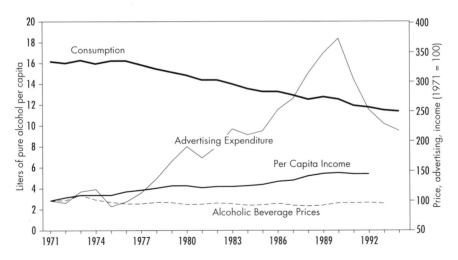

Note: alcoholic beverage prices, advertising expenditures and per capita income are adjusted for inflation and are indexed, with data for 1971 set equal to 100.
Data sources are listed in Calfee (1996), *op cit.*

---

135 See Tim Ambler (1996) 'Can Alcohol Misuse Be Reduced by Banning Advertising?' 15 *International Journal of Advertising*, pp 167–174.

136 Calfee (1996), *op cit*; this was an update from an earlier analysis in Calfee and Sheraga (1994), *op cit.*

Statistical analysis confirmed that advertising has had no discernable effect in increasing French total alcohol consumption above what it would otherwise be. Of course, market shares have shifted (wine's share has fallen dramatically, for example), and advertising is presumably a factor in these shifts. But advertising has had no detectable effect on the deeper issue of how much drinking occurs overall.

The French experience is not unique. In fact, it is typical. Recent statistical analyses of the alcoholic beverage markets in the US, the UK, the Netherlands and Germany all failed to discover any effect from advertising on total alcohol consumption.[138] Canadian experience is also relevant. A recent study by scholars at Ontario's Addiction Research Foundation sought to understand why their province had seen two decades of consistent progress in reducing alcohol abuse even as consumption declined far less rapidly. They concluded that this progress was due to treatment and other prevention measures, not to controls over alcohol marketing or availability.[139] All these results confirmed the conclusions first reached a decade or more ago by the staffs of the FTC and the Addiction Research Foundation when they reviewed the research then available on the effects of alcohol advertising.[140]

Some have argued that the reason so much research fails to detect an effect from advertising is because it analyzes only relatively small changes in advertising volume, such as occur from year to year in the US and the

---

138 Calfee and Scheraga (1994), *op cit*, provides statistical analyses of Germany, Netherlands and the UK, and reviews the extensive statistical research by others. A more complete review is Joseph C Fisher (1993) *Advertising, Alcohol Consumption, and Abuse: A Worldwide Survey*, Greenwood Press. The most recent and most thorough settlement analysis of the US market is Jon P Nelson and John R Moran (1995) 'Advertising and US Alcoholic Beverage Demand: System-Wide Estimates', 27 *Applied Economics*, pp 1225–1236.

139 Reginald G Smart and Robert E Mann (1995) 'Treatment, Health Promotion and Alcohol Controls and the Decrease of Alcohol Consumption and Problems in Ontario: 1975–1993', 30/3 *Alcohol and Alcoholism*, pp 337–343.

140 See Federal Trade Commission, Bureau of Economics and Bureau of Consumer Protection (1985) *Recommendations of the Staff of the Federal Trade Commission Re: Omnibus Petition for Regulation of Unfair and Deceptive Alcoholic Beverage Advertising and Marketing Practices*, Docket No 209–46, p 2: there is 'no reliable basis to conclude that alcohol advertising significantly affects consumption.' The Addiction Research Foundation article is Reginald Smart (1988) 'Does Alcohol Advertising Affect Overall Consumption? A Review of Empirical Studies', 49/4 *Journal of Studies on Alcohol*, pp 314–323.

UK. This appears to leave open the possibility that severe restrictions, such as a complete ban on advertising, would still have strong and visible effects on consumption.[141] The French data refute this view. France has seen dramatic increases *and decreases* in advertising volume. Also relevant is the Dutch experience. Starting in 1991, advertising expenditures simultaneously skyrocketed in the Netherlands and plummeted in France. In both nations, however, the downward paths in consumption continued as before, and statistical analysis revealed no impact from advertising in either nation.[142]

Why Doesn't Advertising Increase Consumption, and Why Do Sellers Advertise Anyway?

How can it be that large expenditures on advertising fail to increase overall consumption of alcoholic beverages? One way to answer this is by making a distinction between 'new' and 'mature' markets. A new market is one in which a product category, such as digital audio tape players, is unfamiliar to consumers. Advertising's purpose in a new market is to provide information about general product attributes, including the uses and benefits of the entire product category. Advertisers stimulate demand for a product category as a by-product of enhancing demand for their own brands.

As product awareness spreads, the need for emphasizing overall product attributes declines (unless there are dramatic new developments in the product itself). At this point, consumers have largely made up their minds about whether to use the product at all, and their usage decisions come to rely upon information from friends and other sources rather than from advertising. The market has become mature. Mature markets are characterized by a proliferation of brands and sub-brands, most of them supported by advertising. But economic theory, plus extensive scientific research, indicates that advertising in a mature market – such as that for alcoholic beverages, detergent soaps, or toothpaste – does little or nothing

---

141 See Henry Saffer (1995) 'Alcohol Advertising and Alcohol Consumption: Econometric Studies', in Susan Martin, ed, *The Effects of the Mass Media on the Use and Abuse of Alcohol*, Research Monograph No 28, pp 83–99.

142 Calfee and Scheraga (1994), *op cit*, and Calfee (1996), *op cit*.

to increase total demand. Rather, advertising serves to develop and maintain brand loyalty. In other words, advertisers in a mature market compete for a share of existing customers, so that the effect of advertising is to cause roughly offsetting shifts in market share among winning and losing brands.[143]

Then why bother to advertise at all? The answer is competition. Each firm advertises its brands in the belief (almost certainly true) that to cease advertising is to concede the market to the competition. The result can easily be a stand-off, with much battling over market shares and no effect on total market demand.

By misunderstanding this simple reasoning, some commentators have perpetuated a basic error when discussing the effect of advertising on total market sales. It is an elementary fallacy in economic reasoning to assume that just because each firm does better with advertising than without, it must be true that the market as a whole does better.[144] An obvious example is political advertising. Each candidate believes advertising is necessary, and each one does it in the hope of increasing his own vote. Total advertising expenditures accordingly increase year after year (except, as a general rule, where this is prohibited by law). But there is no reason to think this causes more people to vote.

Clearly, we can dispense with the old idea that more advertising necessarily implies more consumption. That has been refuted by economic reasoning and carefully documented experience. Ad bans therefore do not reduce consumption of controversial products such as tobacco or alcohol. Rather, bans suppress information and inhibit competition. They impede competitive processes that provide consumers with useful information

---

143 For academic analyses of the mature market concept and the role of advertising, see Henry Grabowski (1978) 'The Effects of Advertising on the Intraindustry Distribution of Demand', *Explorations in Economic Research* (Occasional Papers of the National Bureau for Economic Research), 4, pp 675–701, and PW Kyle, (1982) 'The Impact of Advertising on Markets', 1/4 *Journal of Advertising*, pp 345–359. A widely used textbook treatment is Charles Patti and Charles Frazer (1988) *Advertising: A Decision-Making Approach*, Dryden Press. A recent systematic empirical study of numerous mature markets is Jo Yasin (1995) 'The Effects of Advertising on Fast-moving Consumer Goods Markets', reprinted from the *International Journal of Advertising* in Luik and Waterson (1996), *op cit.*

144 Ricardo Caballero (1992) 'A Fallacy of Composition', 82/5 *American Economic Review*, pp 1279–1292.

about products, even including negative information that harms the industry but is valuable to consumers (see chapter 3 on less-bad advertising). Bans also retard the worldwide movement toward 'lighter' products with less fat and cholesterol, less alcohol and less tar and nicotine.

In view of such a discouraging record for ad bans, it is only natural to think about less restrictive approaches to advertising. One is self-regulation, an important but neglected topic.

6 Self-Regulation

*'The dishonest advertiser is a menace to honest business and the public.
Every time people are misled by an advertisement ..., honest advertisers
are injured.'* [145]

Advertising self-regulation is an odd topic in the economics of advertising.
It is an ancient activity, much older than formal regulation. It takes on
many forms, and it is much different today than it was just a few decades
ago. Its importance is undeniable, yet almost nothing is known of its effects.
This is unfortunate, because self-regulation can clearly bring both good and
harm to the marketplace. We do know, however, that some nations already
have highly organized self-regulation systems that may confer substantial
gains for consumers.

Advertising self-regulation was once a specialty of trade groups.
Physicians, attorneys, architects and others organized to defend and
promote their professions and not coincidentally, to restrain competition.
They put together codes of ethics, which often restricted or even banned
advertising. That is the kind of thing the FTC has been working to get rid
of for the past two decades. Nowadays, in the US at least, trade groups
either leave advertising alone or adopt standards that are not so clearly
protectionist.

Another kind of self-regulation involves individual media outlets.
By the late nineteenth century, both the *Ladies Home Journal* and *Good
Housekeeping* were monitoring ads and refusing ones that did not meet their
standards. Other magazines and some newspapers have long had less formal
policies (many do not carry cigarette and weapons ads, for example).[146]

---

145 Cole, 'Review of the Ten-Year Fight Against Fraudulent Advertising (part 1)', *Printers Ink*, 24 February
1921, p 18.
146 See Rotzoll, Kim B, and James E Haefner, with Steven R Hall (3rd ed, 1996) *Advertising in
Contemporary Society: Perspectives Toward Understanding*, University of Illinois Press, p 169ff.

A third kind of self-regulation has achieved prominence in recent decades. This is where non-government organizations oversee entire sectors, such as all print advertising. This modern version of self-regulation began fitfully in the 1960s, assumed a substantial role in America and the UK in the 1970s, and soon spread to parts of continental Western Europe. Now it is taking root around the world, including the developing economies of Asia and the emerging post-communist societies of Europe.

Advertising self-regulation has even become a commodity in international trade. Experienced suppliers, notably the International Chamber of Commerce (ICC), with headquarters in Paris, design and export self-regulatory systems to small nations that see no reason to spend their limited funds on re-inventing the wheel. A flotilla of international groups play essential facilitating roles. These include the World Federation of Advertisers (WFA), the European Advertising Tripartite (EAT), and the European Advertising Standards Alliance (EASA), all headquartered in Brussels, and the International Advertising Association (IAA) in New York.[147]

In theory, advertising self-regulation groups can provide standards, accept complaints from consumers and competitors, resolve the bulk of complaints quickly and quietly, work with outside experts to resolve most of the rest, marshal adverse publicity in the few instances in which an advertiser resists the organization's decision and finally, turn the handful of remaining cases over to government authorities.

That is roughly how things work in the US and the UK, except that the American broadcast networks pre-clear their own ads, and the UK self-regulation system leaves broadcast advertising to the government-sponsored Independent Television Commission. All these self-regulation bodies establish general guidelines for advertising truthfulness and content, along with more specific rules for certain products (such foods or alcohol) and certain advertising practices (such as comparisons). The rules are

---

147 Jean Boddewyn, a long-time student of advertising self-regulation, provides a thorough review in *Global Perspective on Advertising Self-Regulation,* Quorum Books (1992). The World Federation of Advertisers, in Brussels, provides regular updates in their publications, as does the International Chamber of Commerce, located in Paris. A recent overview, from a somewhat legal perspective, is provided by Petty (1997), *op cit.*

typically quite strict for sensitive products such as alcohol, tobacco, foods, and toys or anything else involving children.

Other European systems are notable for their diversity. German self-regulation, for example, is concerned almost entirely with matters of taste or opinion. This reflects the law on advertising claims. German law prohibits virtually any claims about 'value,' including sale prices or price comparisons, and strongly discourages virtually any form of comparison claims. It is relatively simple to initiate litigation against advertising claims that violate these rules or that violate more general laws against deceiving consumers, and it is easy to obtain injunctions to halt offending ads. The central issue of consumer deception is often settled with consumer research (rare among European nations), but the government enforces what might be called a 'gullible consumer' standard: a violation occurs if as few as 10% of consumers could be misled by a claim. This legal environment leaves little for self-regulation to do in Germany. [148]

France and Italy, each in their own way, lie somewhere between the extremes of the UK and Germany. The Scandinavians, however, have essentially done away with self-regulation altogether, replacing it with consumer ombudsmen who are government employees.

Why Self-Regulation?

Where does the modern self-regulation movement come from? One source is a concern about the credibility of advertising. This is hardly new, as illustrated in the quotation at the start of this chapter. Advertisers have often complained that obviously false or exaggerated ads can cast doubts on the truth of all advertising. In the early years of this century, the main culprit was often thought to be the so-called patent medicines. These were unregulated, and little was known of their effectiveness or even what they contained. The trade magazine *Printers Ink,* representing the views of the larger and more respectable advertisers, concluded that self-regulation was impossible. It therefore inaugurated a 'truth in advertising' campaign with the goal of obtaining federal and state legislation against false or misleading claims. This campaign was unsuccessful, and little legislation of consequence

---

148 Petty (1997), *op cit.*

emerged despite continued pressure from the advertising industry through the 1920s. Congress did create the FTC in 1914, but primarily to deal with antitrust issues. Its influence on advertising during the next two decades was slight.

This early lack of success should not obscure the essential point. The advertising profession has always been worried about the credibility of advertising, and with good reason. It was their own poll data in the 1930s that first revealed in a scientific manner the fact that consumers are consistently and fundamentally suspicious of advertising (see chapter 2).

Another motivation for self-regulation is quite different, and it is characteristic of economies in the second half of the 20th century. This is the desire to forestall legislated controls and government bureaucracies. Most people probably think that forestalling regulation is the only motivation for self-regulation. It is not, because the desire to enhance credibility is always a factor. But certainly the threat of legislation is central. Advertising self-regulation as we know it arrived in the early 1970s, when advertising faced a threat of onerous regulation in the US and the UK.

Critics of advertising sometimes oppose self-regulation precisely because it is designed to forestall further regulation. Essentially, their argument is that self-regulation in its modern form is merely a weaker and altogether inferior substitute for government regulation. This view is very much mistaken. There is not the slightest doubt that formal regulation often goes too far and therefore victimizes consumers. To state that self-regulation is less intense than government regulation is to praise it more than damn it. Moreover, this is an area where private means have great advantages over regulatory bureaucracies. A few details about how self-regulation operates will illustrate some of the advantages of self-regulation over more formal arrangements.

How Advertising Self-Regulation Works

The chief advertising self-regulation group in America is the National Advertising Division of the Council of Better Business Bureaus. The NAD monitors ads, accepts complaints, and enforces rules established by the FTC or the Council of Better Business Bureaus. It also operates the Children's Advertising Review Unit (with its own guides and with funding from major toy manufacturers) and the National Advertising Review Board (NARB). The latter consists largely of outside experts who attempt to resolve differences that remain after exhausting the NAD's in-house efforts. The handful of cases that defy resolution (typically one or two per year) are sent to FTC. The television networks also operate in-house review systems, whose standards are largely but not completely consistent across networks.[149]

Self-regulation in Europe works in diverse ways. One might think that with such strict advertising regulations in major European nations such as Germany, there is little for European self-regulation groups to do (with the notable exception of the UK, which will be discussed shortly). This is not true. For one thing, the opening up of East European economies is bringing a host of new self-regulation schemes. The Czechs have created a plan closely modeled on the UK system, while Croatia, Poland, Hungary, Russia and the Baltic states are all moving towards other variants of self-regulation.[150]

Equally important, the growth of economic integration in the European Union, combined with advances in transportation and communication technology, has brought a flood of cross-border advertising. The inevitable result is a steady supply of cross-border consumer complaints and disputes among competitors. This has generated a good deal of work for EASA, which handles cross-border complaints and resolves disputes.

Europe is not the only expansionary area for self-regulation. In Asia and Latin America, advertising trade groups are advocating self-regulation as a means for preserving freedom for commercial speech. Systems have been operating for some time in Brazil, Chile, and a few smaller economies, with newer programs in Argentina, Mexico and other nations. As in Eastern Europe, these developments are part of the larger trend toward privatization and liberalized economies.[151]

149 Again, a recent summary is Petty (1997), *op cit.*
150 *WFA Focus*, Issue 30, 1997, discusses the growing participation of Eastern European nations, including the Czech Republic.
151 'SILEC hails benefits of ad self-regulation' *Advertising Age International*, June 1996.

The most elaborate and arguably the most effective self-regulation system in the world operates in the UK. A Committee of Advertising Practice (CAP) was established in 1961 to construct advertising and promotion codes for major industries. The Advertising Standards Authority (ASA) was established the following year to administer the CAP codes for all media except broadcasting. CAP's activities came to include providing pre-publication advice to advertisers who seek it and the vetting of all cigarette advertising.

The ASA enforces the CAP's codes. Funded by a 0.1% assessment on print media and direct mailers, and overseen by a council whose members are mainly drawn from outside the advertising industry, the ASA employs a staff from which attorneys are conspicuously absent. Its job is to monitor advertising and promotion, field complaints and resolve disputes. The ASA's enforcement sanctions are substantial, consisting of adverse publicity, a recommendation (often followed) that media refuse space for offending ads, withdrawal of 'trading privileges' normally available through the CAP and finally, referral of the matter to the government's Office of Fair Trading, with its formal enforcement powers. The link between the ASA and the government is concrete, for the Director of Fair Trading can seek an injunction on the basis of an ASA ruling.[152]

The ASA staff regularly publishes critical surveys of ads from entire industries. Most focus on traditionally controversial industries such as alcohol, health and beauty, weight loss ('slimming' products), and weapons. These reports rate the acceptability of the individual ads and provide useful snapshots of advertising style and content.

The heart of the ASA system is the handling of complaints, which arrived at the rate of 12,000 a year in 1995 and 1996. The vast majority comes from consumers rather than from competitors (the situation is the reverse for the NAD in the US). This massive volume reflects an active marketing effort by ASA itself ('How Dare They!' was the headline for one ASA ad encouraging consumers to complain about ads that make them

---

152 ASA materials are readily available from the ASA's Internet site: www.asa.org.uk. The 1997 article by Petty describes the injunctive role of the Director of Fair Trading.

'angry'). Detailed monthly reports of complaints and their disposition are issued with considerable publicity.

The intended result is a system in which consumers feel they can gain satisfaction regarding ads they do not like (no actual deception or loss is necessary), sellers can expect vindication when complaints are without merit, and truthful ads can work their magic without hindrance from boatloads of false claims. Whether anything like this is actually the result of this self-regulation plan appears to be unknown. So far as I can tell, no one has researched the topic. But then no one has actually demonstrated that the FTC's considerable regulatory clout has made American advertising more credible, either.[153]

To give an idea of how this system works, in 1996 the ASA received 12,055 complaints about 8,409 advertisements. After eliminating complaints that arose from misunderstandings or odd interpretations, about half were investigated. This yielded 720 ads that were deemed to violate one of the codes and were altered or withdrawn; but only 85 ads were asked to be withdrawn on the grounds that they were (in the ASA's words) 'likely to cause serious or widespread offense.' Roughly a fourth of all complaints pertained to taste and decency, which the ASA assesses along with accuracy.

What kind of advertising generates the most complaints? Not what you might expect. The great issues in public disputes over advertising, the targets of ad bans and proposed bans, have little presence in the ASA's lists of most-complained-about ads. Here, in descending order, is a list of the ten most complained-about ads in 1996 (bear in mind that only about half of these complaints were upheld by the ASA): a sexist and otherwise offensive lingerie ad; a distasteful political campaign ad; an overly sexy ad for a sport utility vehicle; a vulgar ad for a minor brand of beer; a clothing manufacturer's ad containing an offensive photograph; an offensive ad for a video game;

---

153 The 'How Dare They' ad is reproduced on p 209 of David Ogilvy (1985), *op cit.* The credibility data reviewed in chapter 2 provide no basis for thinking consumer credibility in advertising increased when FDA regulation increased; see the 1994 Calfee and Ringold article cited in that chapter. Two economists have argued, however, that an extremely indirect test suggests a positive effect from the FTC on advertising credibility. See R Sauer and K Leffler (1990) 'Did the Federal Trade Commission's Advertising Substantiation Program Promote More Credible Advertising?', 80/1 *American Economic Review*, pp 191–203.

a vulgar ad for shoes; an ad for a major cigarette manufacturer on the risks of second-hand cigarette smoke; a vulgar ad for a soft drink; and a sexist public service ad for an advocacy group. Only the tobacco company ad, arguably a political statement, pertained to the topics the are usually at the center of debate of advertising, regulation and ad bans. None of this material is confidential; it is all available from ASA reports and their Internet web site (www.asa.org.uk).

Clearly, the main issues for consumers are taste, propriety and the like, rather than deception or unfairness. One of the most important lessons from the UK self-regulation system, then, is that the concerns of activist groups (alcohol, tobacco, children deceived into harassing their parents) are very different from the concerns of the general public.

Self-Regulation and Consumer Welfare

Can advertising self-regulation be harmful to consumers? The answer depends, surprisingly, on regulatory authorities. If the authorities are sufficiently alert to the anti-competitive elements of self-regulation, they can try to root out the harm and leave the benefits. Then the self-regulation organizations can proceed to conduct investigations in a non-confrontational fashion without the costs and delay of litigation and without the organizational inefficiencies endemic to all government entities.

Of course, there is not a lot to be done when government regulation is too stringent to begin with. German advertising law, for example, is thoroughly hostile to competition through advertising. Its prohibitions on comparative claims and almost any form of price advertising are hardly pro-consumer. This leaves the self-regulation groups with little to do except monitor adherence to the details of the legal code. No wonder German self-regulation is dominated by lawyers, while Britain's ASA is resolute in its dependence on non-attorneys.

The advantages of self-regulation are numerous and compelling. The most obvious is efficiency. This is more than just doing the same thing for less money. The tasks of self-regulation groups are fundamentally different from those of government agencies. Behind-the-scenes negotiation and settlement are cheaper than subpoenas, depositions and lawsuits. The relatively small staffs of the ASA and the US Better Business Bureau's

National Advertising Division will never have to decide, as the FTC routinely does, whether to authorize continuation of a single investigation *after* the legal staff has spent 2,000 attorney-hours (!) on that one inquiry. Private groups also have the luxury of being able to decide individual cases without having to worry about establishing fixed legal precedent. This reduces the opportunities for firms to latch onto fixed principles and use them to gain advantage over their competitors. (Of course, flexible principles can also present opportunities for playing the system against an opponent; the key is reasonable decision-making by independent entities.)

Self-regulation is also closer to the public, that is, closer to the consumers whose interests should be at the heart of the regulatory enterprise. Constructing a complaint system, making it available to consumers, and explaining what it can do and how to use it, comprises a formidable marketing task. It should be no surprise that the experienced self-regulation groups of the US and especially, the UK, are better at this than government lawyers are. Handling some 12,000 complaints per year, almost always with a satisfactory resolution, the ASA seems to command substantial respect from the public.

This success presumably stems partly from the ASA's persistently commonsense and non-legal approach, and it may well bolster advertising credibility and the benefits such credibility brings for buyers and sellers alike. The upshot is that entire regions of the British advertising enterprise are practically devoid of serious criticism from individual consumers. This is true, for example, of alcohol and tobacco advertising (although criticism from health advocates and anti-advertising activists is vehement and unceasing).[154]

In today's global economy, the ability to negotiate outside the shadow of the law has an importance that extends beyond national boundaries. The European Advertising Standards Alliance has performed an important, and perhaps essential, role in adjudicating disputes about cross-border advertising. One shudders to think of what would happen if all these issues had to be decided by one of the Directorates of the European Commission (or worse, by *several* EC Directorates).

---

154 *Cf* the ASA's annual reports.

Just as self-regulation groups are closer to the consumer, they are also closer to the industry. The point is not that self-regulation supports the industry – the ASA is known for strict enforcement of its codes for alcohol, tobacco and pharmaceuticals – but that self-regulation can apply the knowledge that such closeness brings. Government agencies, on the other hand, are famous for their apparent inability to understand how advertising works.

I noted that in the past few years, many nations have been adopting new, or in most cases, their first advertising self-regulation institutions. The list includes Mexico, Poland, the Czech Republic, the Baltic nations, Russia, Croatia, and Thailand. This is an interesting list. It bears a striking resemblance to the list of economies emerging from decades of communism, socialism, or state-directed autocracy. Advertising self-regulation can be seen as one of the many systems and institutions that are sweeping through newly liberated economies.

7 Some Lessons for Advertising Regulation

'We Try Harder'[155]

More than three decades of research have transformed our understanding of competitive advertising. Two broad findings stand out. First, advertising has an unsuspected power to improve consumer welfare. As a market-perfecting mechanism, advertising arises spontaneously to attack serious defects in the marketplace. Advertising is an efficient and sometimes irreplaceable mechanism for bringing consumers information that would otherwise languish on the sidelines. Advertising's promise of more and better information also generates ripple effects in the market. These include enhanced incentives to create new information and develop better products. Theoretical and empirical research has demonstrated what generations of astute observers had known intuitively, that markets with advertising are far superior to markets without advertising.

The second finding is that competitive advertising is fundamentally a self-correcting process. Some people may find this surprising. Well-informed observers once thought that unregulated advertising would bring massive distortion of consumer information and decisions. Careful research, however, has shown these fears to be groundless. Self-correcting competitive forces in advertising generate markets in which information is richer and more fundamentally balanced than can be achieved through detailed controls over advertising and information.

Here are some implications for the regulation of advertising. It will be seen that we should fear regulation far more than we should fear persuasion.

---

155 International slogan for Avis car rental, banned in Germany because it denigrated the market leader, acording to Petty (1997), *op cit*, p 7.

Why it is Easy to Over-Regulate Advertising

The richness and subtlety of competitive advertising provide endless opportunities for harmful regulation based upon misconceptions of how advertising works. For example, we should avoid the mistake of assuming that the highly incomplete nature of information in advertising will lead to consumer deception. Advertising must supply information in bits and pieces. The very sparseness of information in ads is what provides the agility necessary for the give-and-take of vigorous competition. Improvements in the marketplace come step-by-step through small increments in information. It was the concise 'Think small' imagery in VW's ads, not a raft of mechanical details, that disrupted the American car market in the 1960s and forced other manufacturers to hew more closely to what consumers wanted. With health claims for foods, most progress came through incremental shifts in emphasis, from fat to saturated fat to cholesterol, and on to fiber and then soluble fiber and so on, all with small improvements in the products themselves.[156]

Thus one lesson is to restrain our natural suspicion of the highly incomplete nature of advertising. If ads are forced to 'tell the whole story' (as some would have it), advertising will be more expensive, less competitive, and ultimately less informative because most information would disappear altogether in a desperate attempt to avoid incomplete information. Providing information in bits and pieces is one of advertising's cardinal virtues, not a flaw. And it is inevitable. Look at advertising by individuals and groups who count themselves as critics of advertising. Political advertising, whether by free-market advocates or socialists, routinely resorts to provocative slogans and the most abbreviated analysis of issues and opponents. Promotional literature for advocacy groups such as America's militantly anti-advertising Center for Science in the Public Interest lures subscribers and contributors with numerous non-FDA-approved claims about how foods and vitamins can prevent disease. If grossly incomplete information in advertising is deceptive, then practically all fund-raising campaigns by activist groups are deceptive.

156 See the second section of chapter 2

Unfortunately, the temptation to think that advertising is deceptive is always present. People tend to think that *other* people are fooled by what they themselves understand perfectly. This is an example of the well-documented 'third-person' effect. A good example is a recent Canadian survey. Seventy-six percent agreed 'advertising is often misleading,' but only 15% agreed that 'I am frequently misled by advertising.'[157]

There is another trap that regulators fall into: assuming that ads imply a 'false uniqueness' when, for example, one brand of vegetable oil advertises 'no cholesterol' even though that is true of all vegetable oils. The FDA once expanded this elementary error into a new initiative in the regulation of promotional messages on food labels. That was in 1991, when the FDA ordered vegetable oil manufacturers to stop making 'no cholesterol' claims.[158] The FDA understood that the absence of cholesterol in vegetable oil was a useful fact for consumers to know, but it missed the crucial point. If sellers cannot attach a valuable piece of information to their own brands, they have little incentive to provide it to consumers.

The FDA threw the baby out with the bathwater when it removed incentives for entire food categories to use brand advertising to promote the health benefits of that category. I have been told that a famous American chicken grower was once advised that he should refrain from advertising that his brand of chicken had less fat and cholesterol than beef, unless his ads also pointed out that all brands of chicken have less fat and cholesterol than beef. 'Why should I advertise my competition?' he asked, and dropped his plans for fat and cholesterol advertising.[159]

Unfortunately, the FDA never has grasped this lesson. After it revamped health claims regulation to make it nearly impossible to make a health claim for just a single brand instead of an entire product category,

---

157 Crane (1991), *op cit*, Table 1. On the third-person effect in the context of advertising, see Albert C Gunther and Esther Thorson (1992) 'Perceived Persuasive Effects of Product Commercials and Public Service Announcements: Third-Person Effects in New Domains', 19 *Communication Research*, p 574. A similar effect in a very different context is described in Marilyn Jacobs Quadrel, Baruch Fischhoff and Wendy Davis (1993) 'Adolescent (In)vulnerability', 48/2 *American Psychologist*, pp 102–116.

158 See John E Calfee, 'FDA Underestimates Food Shoppers', *Wall Street Journal*, 29 May 1991, p A10.

159 The grower was Frank Perdue, colorful proprietor of Perdue's Chickens, which were sold under that brand supported by vigorous advertising.

we began to see newspaper headlines like, 'It's Good for You – But Don't Expect Foods Labels to Say That,' and 'Consumers Overcome Their Food Guilt: Research shows beef, butter, fat slipping back into Americans' diet.' Health claims practically ceased to exist for several years, and consumer awareness of diet and health began to regress to what it had been before health claims arrived.[160]

Another essential lesson is that it is a mistake to assume that regulation is necessary to force advertising to tell consumers what is wrong with a product. 'Less-bad' advertising is endemic in markets – unless regulation prohibits comparative claims, of course. This is clear from the history of advertising for products ranging from cigarettes and automobiles to foods and life insurance. We can dismiss the idea that regulation is necessary to get advertising to move beyond purely positive claims. Experience shows that in comparison to regulatory requirements for disclosures, balance, and so forth, 'less-bad' advertising is a far more compelling and consumer-friendly mechanism for getting fuller information into the marketplace.

In fact, regulation can *stop* competitive advertising from providing negative information about a product. It was the 1960 FTC prohibition on tar and nicotine claims that motivated *Printers Ink*'s rhapsodic description of the suddenly pure cigarette ads with their depictions of 'flavor, taste and pleasure against a backdrop of beaches, ski slopes and languid lakes' (see chapter 3).

All this means that it is very easy for regulation to go too far. After all, vigorous regulation must do something the market does not do by itself, or regulators look silly. If the market already provides what is most essential to consumers, it follows that vigorous regulation is bound either to wipe out useful claims or burden them with unnecessary requirements.

---

160 On the FDA rules and their implications, see Ippolito and Mathios (1993), *op cit.* The first headline is from the *Los Angeles Times* (8 May 1995), *op cit.* The article notes, 'The lack of boastfulness among food producers [about health benefits of fiber, calcium, etc.] is one of the unexpected results of federal food labeling reforms, which are a year old today.' The second headline is from *Advertising Age*, 2 May 1994, p S–6, which also says, 'Nutritional concerns about cholesterol, salt, preservatives, sugar, caffeine and additives have fallen sharply since 1990, the height of America's healthy food craze, [a recent] study shows.'

Perhaps the most striking example of how this can happen involves the most fundamental negative information of all: price.

A case study: price claims in advertising

Many nations have restricted price claims. Almost never are the restrictions limited to simple price comparisons like '$100 off' or '10% less than usual price.' Firms eager to cut prices find more subtle ways to communicate their intentions to their customers. Consumers learn this, watch for signals, and pretty soon a price war is in the works. A recent Supreme Court decision overturning a ban on price advertising was triggered by a competitor's complaint about a claim that consisted of the word 'WOW.' The ad contained no price at all for the product in question (which was liquor, for which price ads were prohibited). The competitor knew that even a vague reference to price-cutting would initiate a process that could only lead to lower prices.[161]

Prohibitions on price comparison claims are often justified on the grounds that the claims are usually deceptive in one way or another. The problem with this approach is that an energetic chase after *possible* deception will eventually cause *certain* harm to consumers. This happens because price claims are part of a process, not isolated events. That is why they are so feared by competitors.

This point is worth exploring by looking more closely at how regulators often deal with price comparison ads such as '30% off the list price,' '20% of our usual price,' 'reduced 40%,' or maybe 'lowest prices in town.' These are called 'reference price' ads because they contain some kind of comparison price as a reference. In chapter 2, I mentioned that the FTC quit attacking these kinds of claims at the very time it was *expanding* its advertising regulation in response to demands from consumer groups and others. Here are the reasons for that switch in policy.

Historically (in the US at least), regulation of price comparisons has been just one step in a sequence of events. The typical course of events runs like this. Price claims invite comparison shopping. This puts pressure on

---

161 The case was *44 Liquormart, Inc, et al v Rhode Island*, 13 May 1996, which is discussed in chapter 8. The ad did contain prices for other products.

competitors. They tend to respond in one of two ways: they either lower their own prices or they try to persuade regulatory authorities to stop the other guys' price advertising. You can guess which is their first choice; they talk to the regulators.

Having thus been called to attention, regulators soon observe certain irregularities in the price ads. Sellers cannot know how well a product will sell at its original price, so they often have to reduce their prices. Then they need to tell consumers what they have done, so a 'sale' or '% off' ad is in order. If the new price works, the retailer will sell a lot more than it did at the original price. This looks suspicious. Maybe the seller didn't expect to sell at the original price and only used it as a pretext for a sale. There is no way to know for sure. If the ads compare prices to a 'list price' or to the prevailing price among competitors, their comparisons may become outdated after competitors respond by reducing their own prices. Either way, something seems amiss.

Now, three things are happening. First, the one doing the price advertising is the price cutter. Second, buyers are getting better deals because the market is becoming more competitive as price cuts spread. And third, the 'reference' price (i.e., the original price, list price, etc.) looks like a 'fictitious' price – precisely because the price competition caused by the ads have made the reference prices obsolete.

That explains why the FTC spent so much of its energy in the 1950s and 1960s on 'fictitious price' cases, always with the support of the advertiser's competitors. The FTC always thought it could find some kind of deception going on. But the litigation impeded the shift toward more efficient retailers who charged lower prices and wanted their customers to know it.

By 1970, the FTC had finally caught on to what was happening. One of the architects of the renewal of the FTC in the early 1970s (then Bureau of Consumer Protection director and now Chairman of the FTC Robert Pitofsky) noted in 1977 that the FTC had stopped bringing fictitious pricing cases some eight years earlier, and for very good reasons. The price claims tended to be 'innocuous, either because consumers are in a position to check the validity of exaggerated claims (for example, where comparison shopping is relatively simple) or because the claims are so unlikely ('lowest price ever') or ambiguous ('10% off') that they will be ignored by almost all consumers.' Pitofsky also noted that '… as long as consumers are accurately informed of the offering price, they can make sensible decisions, and the transactions may still be at prices lower than could be obtained at most other outlets in the marketing area.' And finally the bottom line: '[M]uch fictitious pricing enforcement entails considerable social and economic costs. A natural target for such enforcement has been discount houses, and the usual complainants have been nondiscounters who emphasize service and reliability rather than price. Aggressive enforcement against discounters that forces them to hew close to the line of accurate information may tend to dampen competitive activity.' [162]

A more instructive example of how misconceived regulation hurts consumers could hardly be imagined. One can only hope that as the EU proceeds through the harmonization process for borderless commerce, it will increase the pressures to do away with the misguided prohibitions against price advertising now in force in several nations – along with prohibitions on other forms of comparative advertising.

Why Advertising Bans Are Anti-Consumer

Ad bans have political appeal for all the wrong reasons. Entrenched companies and their lobbyists like bans because they protect them against competition from upstarts and outsiders. Politicians like bans because they seem to offer a way to attack social problems without spending tax dollars. Health activists like bans because getting an ad ban demonstrates an ability to 'do something' without actually doing anything constructive at all. And all sorts of people like all sorts of ad bans (toys, alcohol, medicines, and so on) because they think bans might help and do not see how they can hurt.

We know that ad bans do not achieve what they are designed to do – at least, not when they are supposed to reduce alcohol consumption and abuse, cigarette smoking, and the like. We also know that ad bans can hurt. They interfere with giving consumers what they want: better toys, lower prices, less cholesterol, drinks with lower alcohol content (or maybe fruit

---

162 Pitofsky (1977), *op cit*, pp 687–688.

juices or soft drinks), western-style filter cigarettes, prescription drugs with fewer side effects. A lot of times, this happens just because domestic firms want protection from competition. Consumers seldom understand the stakes in an ad ban, however, because advertising's best work often arrives through circuitous routes that escape the attention and understanding of most people. It is advertising aimed at *children* that causes *retailers* to offer more toys at lower prices *paid by adults.*

Always remember this: if an ad ban is not keeping sellers from providing what buyers want, it is not doing its job.

Why Advertising Should Be Regulated by Agencies That Understand Advertising

It may seem unnecessary to say that advertising should be regulated by agencies staffed by experts in economics and advertising. Could it be otherwise? In fact, it often is. Health agencies, in particular, have been granted (or have arrogated to themselves) a large and growing role in the regulation of advertising. In America, the FDA has been assigned to regulate prescription drug advertising, over-the-counter drug labels, and food labels. In addition, it has exercised strong influence on over-the-counter drug advertising (where the FTC generally defers to FDA advice on what claims to allow) and food advertising, where, again, the FTC has often discouraged health claims that have not gone through the FDA's arduous approval process.

For decades, the FDA effectively prohibited health claims in food ads, even though it had no formal jurisdiction over food advertising. It did this by arguing that any health claim whatsoever was equivalent to advertising the food as a drug. The food/drug was then subject to seizure by the FDA on the grounds that the new 'drug' lacked proper labeling on dosage, illnesses being treated, and so on. The FDA even tried to use this cleverly designed legal 'squeeze play' to keep manufacturers from so much as mentioning cholesterol or saturated fat in the 1950s and 1960s, when public health experts were urging consumers to improve their diet in order to prevent heart disease. Manufacturers who tried to convey this advice to consumers immediately met resistance from the FDA. As described in chapter 2, it took courageous action by the FTC, the National Cancer

Institute, and the Kellogg Corporation to end the FDA's chokehold on health claims for foods.[163]

The incursion of health agencies into advertising policy is especially pronounced in connection with tobacco and alcohol. The FDA proposed in 1996 to take over cigarette advertising regulation from the FTC, and it may get its way through its own Rulemaking or through legislation. The recent proposal to ban cigarette advertising in the UK was inspired by the Department of Health. France's notorious loi Evin, which banned tobacco advertising and severely restricted alcohol ads, was named after the Health Minister who mistakenly thought his law would improve health.[164] It has not, of course. Current proposals for EU-wide restrictions or bans are coming from EC Directorates whose principle responsibilities involve health rather than economics.

There are three problems with having health agencies get involved in the economics of advertising. One is that they invariably over-estimate the power of advertising to achieve what advertisers want it to achieve. This misplaced confidence in advertising causes health agencies to want to ban advertising they do not like and to support advertising they do like, such as anti-drug, anti-tobacco and anti-alcohol messages.

When such plans have actually been implemented, the results have generally been disappointing. The disappointment dates back at least twenty-five years. In 1977, two researchers who studied anti-drug messages noted that 'A well-controlled experiment finds that the messages decrease rather than increase negative attitudes toward potentially dangerous drugs,' and added that careful researchers had feared such effects some years earlier. This kind of result has given rise to an entire literature on the so-called 'reactance' phenomenon, in which messages evoke the opposite of the intended response. Nonetheless, the impulse to employ ads and ad bans to improve health continues unabated, as in the case of France's loi Evin.[165]

163 A superb source on the 'squeeze play' and the surrounding events can be found in Peter Barton Hutt (1986) 'Government Regulation of Health Claims in Food Labeling and Advertising', 41 *Food Drug Cosmetic Law Journal*, pp 3–75. The squeeze play is discussed at p 25.

164 See chapter 5.

165 See Lipsitz, Brake, Vincent, and Winters (1993), *op cit*. The quote on anti-drug messages is from P C Feingold and M L Knapp (1977) 'Anti-Drug Abuse Commercials', 27:1 *Journal of Communication*, pp 20–28.

Strange as it may seem, these same health agencies also tend to under-estimate the benefits of advertising. The main reason is a failure to comprehend the dynamics of competition through advertising. When the FDA implemented its new powers over health claims for foods, it constructed rules that completely disregarded the basic economics of competition through advertising. It was as if the FDA had never seen the research on health claims performed by its own staff, the FTC staff and others. The effect of the new rules was to remove virtually all health claims from the market, either by requiring too much substantiation or by insisting that sellers emphasize that their health claims applied to entire food categories rather than just one brand.[166]

This is typical of a larger pattern, the tendency for health agencies to translate their misconceptions about advertising into binding rules. The usual result is to stop useful information while failing to stop harmful habits. The alliance described in chapter 5 between the Chinese tobacco monopoly and anti-smoking activists is an example. Another occurred in 1960, when the FTC succumbed to the advice of the US Department of Health, Education and Welfare (later the Department of Health and Human Services) and prohibited all tar and nicotine information from cigarette advertising. Reductions in tar and nicotine immediately halted. The relentlessly anti-smoking publication *Readers Digest* complained bitterly:

> What Happened to Filter-Tips in 1961–63? The question can be answered in one word: Nothing. The latest laboratory tests … show the tar and nicotine in the smoke of current filter-tip cigarettes to be substantially the same as when the last report was published in July 1961. (The same is true of most popular plain-tip brands – no significant change.)
>
> The reason for this is the Federal Trade Commission 'black-out' of facts and figures in cigarette advertising in 1961. Since no claims of superior or improved filtration can be made, cigarette manufacturers have quit trying to produce 'safer' cigarettes lower in tar and nicotine. Between 1957 and 1960, such competition reduced the tars in American cigarette smoke by 60 percent. When the 'tar derby' ended, so did research for safer cigarettes.[167]

---

166 See Ippolito and Mathios (1996), *op cit.*

167 Report to Consumers', *Reader's Digest*, August 1963, p 99. As I noted in Calfee (1986), *op cit*, later calculations showed that the actual decline was not 60% but about 30–40%.

Nearly a decade passed before federal agencies realized their folly, switched sides and eventually decided to *require* cigarette manufacturers to publicize the very information they had been forbidden to disclose.[168]

Finally, health agencies have a tendency to dispense with the basic regulatory principles employed by agencies that deal exclusively with economic issues. FDA rules for promotional messages on food labels are full of arbitrary prohibitions and requirements bearing no more than a tenuous connection to how consumers actually perceive and use information. The FDA's rules on prescription drug advertising, with the requirement for a 'brief summary' of the detailed labeling information (a summary that not even the FDA claims is absorbed by anyone whatsoever) and the prohibition on any information not formally approved by the FDA (regardless of how well-supported that information is), have absolutely nothing to do with the deception of either physicians or consumers. I hope that the FDA's recent decision to permit television ads without the brief summary will shortly be expanded to include print advertisements.[169]

These three lessons suggest that the consumer's interest lies more with unregulated markets than with regulation. This is not because regulators lack intelligence or goodwill (both of which qualities I have observed in abundance in my dealings with regulatory agencies), but because the system is stacked against them – or more precisely, the system is stacked against wise and beneficial rules. The dynamics of advertising regulation tend to run counter to the public interest for reasons beyond the control of any regulator no matter how well-intentioned.

This suggests taking a hard look at whether markets and consumers would be better off if advertising was granted more freedom.

---

168 This story is recounted in my articles cited in chapter 5.

169 *Washington Post*, 9 August 1997, p A1, 'FDA Relaxes Rules for On-Air Drug Ads', by John Schwartz.

8 Advertising and Freedom

'... commercial messages played such a central role in public life prior to the Founding [of the United States] that Benjamin Franklin authored his early defense of a free press in support of his decision to print, of all things, an advertisement for voyages to Barbados.' [170]

The remarkable passage quoted above describes a pamphlet written by someone we know as an author, scientist and statesmen, but who at the time was just another relentlessly profit-seeking 25-year-old printer. The young Benjamin Franklin apparently saw advertising and free speech as inseparable in the year 1731. So did the US Supreme Court in 1996.

For most of the two and one-half centuries in between, however, advertising was widely believed to have nothing to do with free speech. That changed with the Supreme Court's 1976 Virginia Pharmacy decision, which provided limited protection under the First Amendment's free speech clause to non-misleading advertising. [171] Now, two decades later, many other western nations also provide at least some degree of protection for commercial speech.

Why Protect Commercial Speech?

This development should not be seen as just a matter of multi-billion-dollar enterprises cloaking themselves in protections designed to help spunky newspaper publishers. Constitutional protection for advertising is explicitly based upon the idea that freedom to advertise brings benefits to markets generally, especially to consumers. The central argument in Supreme Court

---

170 From the US Supreme Court's opinion in *44 Liquormart, op cit,* slip opinion, p 8. The quoted passage went on to give the following citation: Franklin, *An Apology for Printers,* 10 June 1731, reprinted in *Writings of Benjamin Franklin,* vol 2, p 172 (1907).

171 *Virginia Citizens Consumers Council, Inc v State Board of Pharmacy,* 373 F Supp 683 (1974), *aff'd,* 425 US 748 (1976).

decisions overturning restrictions on advertising is that consumers can benefit from a free exchange of information – the 'marketplace of ideas' celebrated by authors and jurists since at least the time of John Milton.[172] But even that argument, powerful as it is, falls short of a full understanding of the connections between advertising and free speech.[173]

At least three distinct arguments about advertising and freedom emerge from recent research on the effects of advertising. Each merits attention.

The dynamics of competitive advertising tend to favor consumers over sellers

Advertising fills in information gaps that would otherwise plague markets because there are no property rights to pure information. The benefits to consumers are immense, as is evident from pharmaceutical advertising, health claims in food ads, and price promotions. In each case, the positive spillover effects from competitive advertising appear to swamp the profits gained by the firms actually doing the advertising.

The legal implications may not be obvious to those unacquainted with constitutional law. If most of the benefits from providing valuable information go to someone else, the incentives to provide that information are weak. Potential producers of the information are therefore easily intimidated by government authority. A gross disparity between the value of speech and the incentives to provide it is therefore a classic reason for providing constitutional protections.

We can now see that this reasoning applies to advertising claims as well as to political and artistic expression. Even though advertising as an activity may survive the heavy hand of regulation, the most important *content* of that advertising may disappear without a trace unless regulators are simply

---

172 'Let [truth] and falsehood grapple; who ever knew Truth put to the worse in a free and open encounter?', John Milton, *Areopagitica: A Speech for the Liberty of Unlicensed Printing*, edited by H B Cotterill, 1959, p 6.

173 For a recent insightful review of commercial speech and constitutional issues, see Fred S McChesney (1997) 'De-Bates and Re-Bates: The Supreme Court's Latest Commercial Speech Cases,' 5 *Supreme Court Economic Review*, pp 81–140.

prohibited from suppressing truthful, non-misleading speech. The fact that the dynamics of advertising tend to favor consumers rather than producers is therefore of fundamental legal significance.[174]

Also relevant is a second aspect of competitive advertising. The more aggressive the advertising, the more likely it is to trigger self-correcting market forces. Much of the material in this book illustrates the ways in which pure self-interest causes advertising to focus on the information most needed by consumers even when that information and its effects are contrary to the interests of industry. This is one of the clearest lessons from 'less-bad' claims, price advertising and other episodes. The net result of these tendencies is that when left alone, advertising tends to work to the benefit of consumers even at the sacrifice of advertisers. Advertising therefore tends to promote the public good even without regulation. The implication is that the risks from providing constitutional protection for commercial speech are far less than most people assume.

The dynamics of regulation tend to favor producers over consumers

The natural tendency of advertising regulation, like all regulation, is to reduce competition. Of course, one can easily imagine exceptions. Indeed, the ostensible purpose of advertising regulation it to expand competition by making it easier for consumers to disentangle true and false claims. But experience has shown that regulation often departs from that scenario. The more detailed the regulations, the more likely it is that regulatory minutia are devised and supported by industry, to the harm of consumers. This is clear from, to cite just one example, regulation of price and value claims. More generally, ad bans practically never achieve the social goals set forth by the advocates of the bans. Instead, they tend to reduce consumer choice and raise prices. Ad bans and other restrictions therefore possess a notably anti-competitive flavor.

---

174 This and some of the discussion to follow draw on the following works, not all of which arrive at the conclusions propounded here: Richard Posner (1986) 'Freedom of Speech in an Economic Perspective,' 20 *Suffolk Law Review*, pp 1–54; Ronald H Coase (1974) 'The Market for Goods and The Market for Ideas,' 64 *American Economic Review* (May), p 384; Ronald H Coase (1977) 'Advertising and Free Speech,' 6 *Journal of Legal Studies*, p 1; and Aaron Director (1964) 'The Parity of the Economic Market Place,' 7 *Journal of Law and Economics*, p 1.

An accounting of information released by advertising or suppressed by the lack of it would be lengthy indeed. Topics range from medical treatments and nutrition to toys and attorney services. Nonetheless, this subject has been but lightly explored by researchers. It is difficult to measure what is not there. What we do know is that the suppression of information occurs with surprising ease. The fact that advertising is a commercial venture is no guarantee that the content of advertising will survive government oversight, no matter how useful that content may be. History is full of accounts of multi-billion dollar firms quickly shelving advertising plans that conflict with laws or regulations, without consumers having the slightest hint of what they may be missing.

Hence advertising regulation has an inherent tendency to go too far – just like censorship of political and artistic speech does. This point, too, is illustrated throughout this book. Particularly notable is the fact that as one looks through time or across nations, one observes vast differences in the degree to which advertising content is controlled. Suppose for the moment that the more extreme forms of regulation are really necessary (prohibitions on price claims in Germany, on image advertising for alcohol in France, on tobacco advertising in Norway, on prescription drug advertising practically everywhere). We would then discover egregious harm from advertising in nations without such restrictions. In fact, we find nothing of the kind. Rather, we find that the advertising claims forbidden in one place yield benefits when allowed in another. This is clear evidence that regulation often goes too far.

The problem is that regulation proceeds with a momentum of its own, with little regard to its impact on consumer welfare. As one sifts through the details of, say, regulation of price advertisements, one is struck by the adverse dynamics of regulation from the standpoint of the consumer. The failure to understand these dynamics, especially the failure to comprehend how the competitive market reacts to advertising claims and to regulatory restrictions, is one reason why over-regulation occurs with such ease.

Political speech and commercial speech overlap one another

This gets to the heart of the issue. If unregulated advertising tends to favor consumers and regulation tends to harm consumers, two alternatives are left. One is to place the more severe forms of regulation off-limits to government, i.e., to protect advertising under constitutional law. The other is to rely upon government to sort out good regulation from bad, always in the interests of consumers. The problem here is that governments tend to look after their own power and interests, especially when citizens dare to speak out against government policies. That is why western nations universally protect political and artistic speech from government control, rather than make a vain appeal for governments to use good sense in deciding what materials can be broadcast or published.

A natural question is whether advertising is effectively immune to the problems that make regulation of political speech impossible. The answer is that advertising cannot be so immune. One reason is that commercial speech and political speech easily become intertwined.

A recent landmark US Supreme Court decision illustrates this point. In its *44 Liquormart* decision, the court overturned a law in the state of Rhode Island that prohibited price ads for alcoholic beverages. The law was enforced by the Rhode Island Liquor Control Administration. Transcripts from meetings of the Liquor Control Administration document that liquor retailers constantly searched competitors' ads for price claims, with an eye to getting licenses of offenders revoked.

A lawyer for a retailer that wanted to advertise lower prices asked the board about the possibility of running ads that attacked the price ban itself. The Administrator assumed (no doubt correctly) that consumers would interpret such ads as a signal that the retailer must have low prices. She therefore suggested such ads should probably be avoided because '… I think you are going to cause yourself more harm than good within the industry and more questioning about your licenses, …' [175]

What we have, then, is political speech ('tear down the ban on price ads') being construed and regulated as commercial speech ('lowest prices in town'). Here is another example. In 1984, R J Reynolds, a large cigarette

---

175 'Travel:' a transcript of a 12 December 1992 meeting of Division of Liquor Control Administration, State of Rhode Island. The transcript also records these remarks by the Administrator of the Administrator earlier in the same meeting: 'The phones do not stop ringing and believe me there are people out there looking at 44 Liquors and Douglas Liquors and I think they have a full time job doing it;' '… they are going to look at any way they can to revoke that license.'

manufacturer, ran ads pointing out that the largest controlled study of smoking and heart disease had failed to yield a significant reduction in heart attacks from quitting smoking (which was perfectly true).[176] Urged on by an outraged public health community, the FTC attacked the ad as being commercial speech and therefore subject to its rules on deceptive advertising. After several years of litigation (including a trial judge's ruling for RJR), the firm gave up and relinquished its right to make its point through advertising.[177]

Those were cases in which political speech took on the appearance of commercial speech (to some eyes, at least). A different problem is that even purely commercial speech can arouse political hostility. It is well known that when regulatory agencies have tight control over firms, they can exercise extraordinary control over advertising. The US Securities and Exchange Commission (SEC), for example, essentially dictates the claims that firms can use to promote their stocks and bonds. The effect is more or less a blanket prohibition on traditional advertising claims when marketing securities. The SEC can do this because firms under its jurisdiction do not dare place ads that would arouse the political passions of such a powerful agency. If securities ads were regulated by the FTC, which has no control over such matters as approving new stock issues, firms would quickly challenge such blatantly unjustified rules.[178]

FDA regulation is another example. The FDA's controls over pharmaceutical promotion clearly lie beyond its legislative mandate. The agency gets away with this because it knows that pharmaceutical firms dare not give offense. This was once explained with refreshing frankness in a law review article by one of the FDA's advertising regulators: '… the FDA licenses the prescription drug products subject to its regulation and approves labeling which effectively sets the limits on what may be communicated about product performance. This pervasive involvement

---

176 See 'Dumb like a fox,' *Forbes Magazine*, 12 March 1984, p 54.

177 The reader is invited to read the original journal article publicized by R J R: 'Multiple Risk Factor Intervention Trial: Risk Factor Changes and Mortality Results' (1982) 248 *Journal of the American Medical Association* (24 September), pp 1465–1477. On the FTC case, see *In re R J Reynolds Tobacco Co*, 111 *FTC* 539 (1988).

178 See, for example, the symposium on 'The First Amendment and Federal Securities Regulation,' in volume 20 of the *Connecticut Law Review* (1988).

in the industry's current and future business means that a corporate decision-maker needs to consider more than just the merits of the company's position in the particular advertising dispute at hand. The executive must also weigh how much disagreement with the FDA staff in a current matter might affect future treatment. No such continuing relationship exists between the FTC and any industry.' [179] In other words, advertisements that violate FDA regulations may be construed as a challenge to the integrity of the agency itself, and as such, may invite retaliation in the form of subtle new hurdles and delays in the myriad details of FDA approval of new drugs, manufacturing changes and other matters.[180]

Clearly, the modern regulatory state sets the stage for collisions between commercial speech and political passion. It is now common for regulatory agencies to exercise the kind of control enjoyed by the FDA and the SEC. Such pervasive regulation was much rarer in the 19th century. That may explain why little notice was given to freedom for commercial speech during the 19th and early 20th centuries. Today, the topic is of surpassing importance.

In nations with authoritative regimes, commercial speech can take on political connotations with amazing ease. Already, the famously free press of Hong Kong has encountered the realities of Communist China's view of the press and its role in the economy. The commercial press wants to report accurate information about commercial issues. Such issues include government economic policy and the prospects of Chinese mainland firms, which happen to be owned by the Chinese government. In 1993, a Hong Kong reporter in China was arrested and imprisoned for printing public government economic data that the prosecutors claimed were 'government secrets.' In March 1997, a vigorously anti-establishment Hong Kong newspaper found itself unexpectedly rejected for financing by a bank that clearly was succumbing to pressure from Chinese mainland authorities not to extend financing to objectionable news sources. Now that Hong Kong is

---

179 Quoted from pp 231–232 of Benjamin Fisherow (1987) 'The Shape of Prescription Drug Advertising: A Survey of Promotional Techniques and Regulatory Trends,' 42 *Food Drug Cosmetic Law Journal*, pp 213–236. Fisherow was a member of the small FDA staff devoted to reviewing and regulating pharmaceutical advertising.

180 This point is expanded in J E Calfee (1996) 'The Leverage Principle in FDA Regulation of Information,' *op cit.*

ruled by China, one can imagine how unlikely it is that Hong Kong newspapers, investment analysts and others will advertise their access to data and insider information about Chinese state firms, despite the obvious importance of such information in Hong Kong financial affairs.[181]

We have, then, three dominant patterns: the pro-consumer workings of competitive advertising, the anti-consumer dynamics of government controls, and the progressive intermingling of commercial and political speech. Taken together, these patterns suggest that regulation of commercial speech, like that of political speech, cannot be fully entrusted to governments. This point is the capstone to all the material presented in this book.

A Summing Up: Consumer Welfare and the Freedom to Advertise

This book began with the observation that advertising is governed by certain basic forces, beginning with the manifest self-interest of advertisers and the implacable skepticism of consumers. A rich body of evidence tells us how these forces work out in markets, and what the implications are for the regulation of advertising.

We have learned that consumers have an enormous stake in advertising. Advertising's effects extend far beyond what is immediately apparent. The seller's self-interested efforts to persuade consumers through information are only the starting point, the pebble sending out ripples in a pond. Events quickly move beyond the advertiser's control. Soon enough, there is the dissemination of further information that can either support or undermine the advertiser's goals, the creation of new information altogether, the development of new or improved products to be marketed through information in advertising, and wholesale changes in prices and product mix. Competition insures that the bulk of the benefits goes to buyers rather than sellers. That is, prices go down rather than up, information dwells on what consumers rather than businesses want to see, and competitors are forced willy-nilly to chase after the dollars or marks or pounds or francs of ever-wiser buyers.

---

181 *New York Times*, 25 June 1997, 'On Beijing's Leash, the News in Hong Kong May Lose Bite,' by Nicholas D Kristof.

Most of these ripple effects from advertising are anything but obvious to consumers. The process by which toy advertising directed at children induces lower prices paid by adults is one example. Another is the effort of pharmaceutical firms to finish a clinical trial on cholesterol and heart attacks so it can get on with the job of educating consumers about heart disease prevention, in the hopes of selling more drugs. The consumer's stake in advertising is not only large, it is by its nature little appreciated.

We have also learned that consumers have a stake in the freedom to advertise. This is because the nature of advertising and its political environment virtually guarantee that regulation will go too far. Advertising is a highly visible target for politicians and advocacy groups eager to claim accomplishments and happy to push through measures (such as ad bans) whose harms defy easy measurement. A multitude of businesses and professions also lend support to advertising restrictions because they know that with advertising come the most arduous forms of competition. These circumstances make for one-sided debates. Unfortunately, the fact that most of advertising's benefits are delayed and indirect makes it difficult for even sympathetic observers to understand or explain what is sacrificed through unwise regulation.

Finally, the modern regulatory state makes it nearly impossible for vigorous advertising to avoid offending political authorities, including authorities whose influence over a line of business is so direct that wise business executives will decline to challenge advertising restraints at all. There is a disturbing catalogue of incidents in which political speech is treated as commercial speech (and therefore subject to regulation that would never be applied to political statements) — and also the reverse situation, in which commercial speech evokes a potent political response normally reserved for disputes over political power.

The implications should command our attention. Competitive advertising is stacked in favor of the consumer interest, and the regulatory system is stacked against it. This is not because regulators, politicians and advocacy groups lack wisdom or goodwill. Over-regulation arises inevitably from the odd collision between advertising's indirect effects and the modern apparatus of the state. The evidence demonstrating a general condition of over-regulation is now overwhelming. Perhaps the simplest and most direct piece of evidence is also the most telling. Nations with unusually strict regulation of advertising have failed to provide notable benefits to consumers in comparison to systems in which such regulation is absent. In fact, consumers appear to be better off in regimes without these strict regulations.

All this provides the context for worldwide efforts to ensure at least a measure of constitutional protection for commercial speech. This is an intensely pragmatic, non-ideological movement. It is not simply an attempt to turn developing constitutional law to the favor of an energetic and articulate industry. Rather, the protection demanded for commercial speech reflects concrete research and experience from several decades of close observation of how advertising and regulation actually work.

The parallels between advertising and political speech are surprisingly close. We know that the only way to guarantee that public comment and advocacy will provide a political system eager to please citizens rather than rulers is to remove political speech from regulation altogether. The same lesson applies to advertising. An unmistakable and unassailable protection for reasonably construed, truthful advertising is a minimum condition for more efficient and more beneficial consumer markets.